McKenzie's Companion

Peter Stanway

Cover design by Peter Stanway
McKENZIE'S COMPANION
© 2012 by Peter Stanway
ISBN 0-9839186-7-8
ISBN13 978-0-9839186-7-7
Library of Congress Control Number: 2012942800
Printed in the United States of America and United Kingdom.
RevMedia Publishing, P.O. Box 5172, Kingwood, TX 77325 USA
www.revmediapublishing.com
www.revministries.com
www.revmedianetwork.com
www.revmediatv.com

To contact Peter Stanway: www.peterstanwaybooks.com

DEDICATION

To every true disciple of Jesus Christ

TABLE OF CONTENTS

INTRODUCTION TO THE STUDY

Thank you for purchasing this book containing *McKenzie's Companion* and *Who is McKenzie?* I pray that you will be blessed and your relationship with Jesus Christ will be the better for it. The general purpose of each book is to take the reader on a journey into Christ.

Without Jesus Christ as our Lord and Saviour, we all lived our lives upside down and back to front as is illustrated in the unusual way these books are presented.

McKenzie's Companion is a collection of short, easy to read devotionals that can be read by Christians for personal edification or by curious non-Christians as an exploration of selected scriptures from the bible. Read together, the reader will discover the scriptural context of McKenzie's scenarios in *Who is McKenzie?* and, hopefully, through that, will see how Jesus Christ can be relevant, if not essential, in their own lives.

Who is McKenzie? introduces us to the remarkable McKenzie character. We travel the globe and enter into the fascinating world of McKenzie. It gives us an overview of his enthralling life. McKenzie is intriguing, upright, fearful but hopeful......The truth is that there is a bit of McKenzie in all of us and a bit of all of us in McKenzie.

Group or Individual Study

The chapters of both *McKenzie* books co-relate to each other; in each book, chapter one lines up with chapter one, chapter two with chapter two….and so on. For group or individual study I have included three pertinent questions on a fresh page after each chapter of *McKenzie's Companion* leaving about one-third of the page blank under each question for the answers.

There are some completely blank pages around the middle of the book for personal notes.

With fifty chapters, at one per week, this book will take a year to complete (allowing for two weeks off).

FOREWORD

Congratulations! What you hold in your hands is a potentially life changing tool written by one of the most gifted teachers currently in worldwide ministry. Let me explain….

As we read through and study *McKenzie's Companion/Who is McKenzie?*, obvious and not so obvious character flaws are addressed as seen through McKenzie. While some books like to "study" the character itself, Stanway uses his character as a focal point to lead his readers into self-awareness. It is not good enough to see McKenzie's flaws alone; we must be aware of our own personal shortcomings and address those in order to see true spiritual growth.

While McKenzie the character is entertaining, there is a deeper truth to grasp through this series; without God, there is no order to our lives. Stanway accentuates this message by designing the covers to represent the disorder and chaos present when God is absent. Yet, even as a set, they are still distinguishable as individual books. While both books are designed in one user-friendly format, it makes for a perfect and convenient study series to be used on an individual or corporate level.

It's been a year now since I met Peter Stanway, and that

meeting altered the course of my life forever. What I was introduced to is a passionate man with an unquenchable hunger to see the spiritually poor of the world come to know and embrace God's truth. It became clear to me that Christianity is more than just a label to Stanway as he applies every ounce of spiritual stamina to share the good news about God's love. Because teaching discipleship is a way of life already for Stanway, it is a natural reflection of his ministry to write a book of this substance. He believes in the message of hope, and what other word could fully embrace the revelation of this good news?

If the concepts that are presented are not only contemplated but then put into action, *McKenzie's Companion/Who is McKenzie?* becomes a life changing guide. When you consider that the author is gifted in discipleship and driven with a unique passion for his readers to know and live by truth, you understand why this book becomes one of the most accredited personal study tools available.

As God clearly led Stanway to write a powerful spiritual guide that can implement change, may you, the reader, embrace the truth that without God there is disorder. Through God, however, all things have purpose, direction and yes, perfect symmetry.

Mary Nichelson Editor, Journalist, Talk Show Host – Atlanta, Georgia USA

1

God's Phone Number

Jeremiah 33:3…..Call to me and I will answer you and tell you great and unsearchable things you do not know.

This scripture is sometimes referred to as, 'God's phone number' because it begins: 'call to me and I will answer you'. However, leaving aside that somewhat flippant remark, the truth is if we call out to God He WILL answer us. No matter what our circumstances, no matter what situation we are in, God will answer us and reveal to us awesome things that we do not and would not know if we had not cried out to him.

God is awesome and His plans and purposes for everyone who believes in Him exceed even our wildest dreams.

We do not need to wait until we are desperate. God is waiting for us to call out to Him today. When we enter into intimate dialogue with God, it delights Him to bless us. In reality, this connection between God and us is called prayer.

Prayer is not only matter of words (many or few) it is also an attitude of heart. When our hearts are on fire with compassion for the lost and hurting, we will connect with God in such a way that abundant blessing will be poured out into our lives and all around our lives. Our prayers will be answered.

Lord Jesus, teach us to pray with Your heart. Amen

1 (A) McKenzie had a nightmare? Have you ever had a nightmare, if so, how did you feel?

1 (B) How much do you love God and how much does God love you?

1 (C) Do you make a 'godly' call on a regular basis. Will you make a goal of spending time with God during this week and writing down what He says?

2

Wisdom

Proverbs 11:30 says…… The fruit of the righteous is a tree of life, and the one who is wise saves lives.

Heavenly wisdom, when referred to throughout the Bible, is described like a character analysis of Jesus Christ. This is not what we immediately think of as wisdom but, in reality, Jesus is the manifestation of God's wisdom.

Therefore, when we read this scripture we can see that, indeed, Jesus is the 'tree of life' and He does save lives.

When we are born again and Jesus lives in us, He can work in us to reveal Himself to others. He can work through us to lead others to their salvation.

Let us seek this kind of wisdom that makes Jesus known.

Lord Jesus, make Yourself manifest in us. Amen.

2 (A) McKenzie remembered his father telling him stories. Do you remember any stories from your childhood that impacted you?

2 (B) Jesus came to save lives. Are you saved, if so, how did you get saved?

2 (C) Think of one simple thing you can do next week in order to make a difference in one person's life?

3

Seduction

Proverbs 7:21-22....With persuasive words she led him astray; she seduced him with her smooth talk. All at once he followed her like an ox going to the slaughter, like a deer stepping into a noose....

In this passage, King Solomon talks of seduction as a woman, but seduction can take on many forms. Advertising companies know all about this and they play on our emotions in an attempt to seduce us into buying their client's products.

However, Solomon was indeed speaking of a woman using her charms to seduce a man into doing her will. The same can be equally said of a man towards a woman or, sadly in these days, the act of seduction can take place between members of the same gender. In every case the end is fatal.

If we think of seduction as a metaphor for sin, then the same analogy applies. Fall foul of sin's temptation and the end result is death. It is clear, therefore, that we are to guard against any form of seduction that will lead us astray.

Lord Jesus, help us to stay fixed upon You and Your plan for our life. Amen.

3 (A) Have you ever bought something just because of the advertisement? What did you buy?

3 (B) What is it that seduces you most and how can you combat/counter that seduction?

3 (C) Think of one action you could take this week to reduce that temptation (e.g.- different route to work, turn off TV, don't flirt with that man/woman)

4

Genealogy

Matthew 1:1-17…… Thus there were fourteen generations in all from Abraham to David, fourteen from David to the exile to Babylon, and fourteen from the exile to the Messiah.

It may seem boring to go through long lists of names that mean little or nothing to us, but those names are important. In this case they show us the lineage of Jesus Christ.

Currently, there is a growing curiosity in people wanting to know their family history, their ancestry. How interesting it is to discover where we have come from and perhaps unearth a few surprises in the process!

However, when we come to Jesus and we are born again, our family roots take on a completely new direction. We are adopted into the family of God. We become sons and co-heirs with Christ. We are new creations and our lives are hidden with Christ in God. Our blood-line starts at Calvary's cross.

Oh yes, we still honour our natural parents and, in love, we reach out to our family and friends, but we are no longer conformed to the pattern of this world. Rather, we are being transformed by the power of God.

Lord Jesus, thank You for being our Saviour and our Brother. Ame

4 (A) McKenzie met someone who reminded him of his past. Jesus has dealt with our past. Do you believe that?

4 (B) What is more important - your earthly family or spiritual family and why are they important?

4 (C) What can you do in this coming week to strengthen/encourage someone in your natural family as well as your spiritual family?

5
Scoffers

2 Peter 3:3 says…..Above all, you must understand that in the last days scoffers will come, scoffing and following their own evil desires.

The dictionary defines scoff as: to speak derisively; mock; jeer. This is what is happening more frequently towards Christians in these last days. In reality, however, to be verbally insulted is nothing compared to what is happening with Christians in many parts of the world. Increasingly, Christians are being physically attacked, tortured and killed for their faith. Persecution is on the increase.

Often, scoffers scoff because they feel threatened by what they attack. We know that the driving force behind these attacks is demonic. They come from *spiritual forces of evil in the heavenly realms* (Ephesians 6:12).

Jesus Christ is coming back soon and the devil is shaking in his boots! These are the Last Days. Very soon, Jesus will take all the believers away and those who are killed for their faith will receive a special martyr's crown.

The church is growing stronger, more and more people are turning to Jesus for salvation. Signs and wonders are on the increase as evidence that the power of God is real. In the heat of persecution comes the reward of a stronger body of Christian believers. Our witness is more effective than ever.

Lord Jesus, come soon. Amen.

5 (A) McKenzie felt ignored by the waiter. Have you ever felt ignored and how did you react?

5 (B) Can you think of a more loving way to react that is a better 'Christian witness'?

5 (C) Our lifestyle and our character are part of our Christian witness. What will you do the next time some-one challenges your faith?

6

God Answers Prayer

Acts 12:5-12……. So Peter was kept in prison, but the church was earnestly praying to God for him. The night before Herod was to bring him to trial, Peter was sleeping between two soldiers, bound with two chains, and sentries stood guard at the entrance. Suddenly an angel of the Lord appeared and a light shone in the cell. He struck Peter on the side and woke him up. "Quick, get up!" he said, and the Then the angel said to him, "Put on your clothes and sandals." And Peter did so. "Wrap your cloak around you and follow me," the angel told him.

Peter followed him out of the prison, but he had no idea that what the angel was doing was really happening; he thought he was seeing a vision. They passed the first and second guards and came to the iron gate leading to the city. It opened for them by itself, and they went through it. When they had walked the length of one street, suddenly the angel left him. Then Peter came to himself and said, "Now I know without a doubt that the Lord has sent his angel and rescued me from Herod's clutches and from everything the Jewish people were When this had dawned on him, he went to the house of Mary

the mother of John, also called Mark, where many people had gathered and were praying.

What an amazing passage of scripture. What an awesome answer to prayer. Peter is so caught-up in the supernatural unfolding of these events that, at first, he thinks he is in a vision.

An angel turns up in his prison cell, wakens him and helps him to walk out of his incarceration. They pass the guards, who see neither Peter nor the angel, and go out of the unlocked main gate, through the streets and into the prayer meeting where they were praying for the very thing that happened before they had even finished praying.

Imagine the euphoric jubilation that filled the room just as angelic light had flooded Peter's cell only moments earlier. Our God hears our prayers and He responds. Hallelujah!

Lord Jesus, You have set me free. Amen

6 (A) McKenzie was spared. It was a miracle. Have you ever witnessed a miracle?

6 (B) These scenarios are very dramatic but can you think of instances when God may have helped you in a similar way?

6 (C) How will you know the next time God prompts you? (e.g. take this road, not that road). Read Acts 8:26 and Acts 9:10-11.

7
Honour God

1 Corinthians 6:19-20…..You are not your own; you were bought at a price. Therefore honour God with your bodies.

In these modern times we live in a world of extremes. People who live in the rich Western World are, mostly, living with an obesity problem; whereas, people living in the ravaged Third World are, mostly, living with a famine problem.

In the West, many of us eat too much and we do not exercise enough. Yes, I know that there are some people who are overweight because of health issues, but, for most of us, our busy lives mean that we often eat convenience food on the go. Conversely, our lazy lifestyles often mean we snack junk food between our oversized meals. We are, all too often, guilty of treating our bodies like dustbins into which we put all kinds of rubbish.

Maybe you are neither a couch potato nor a fast living, career-driven executive but the likelihood is (apart from a few health-focussed individuals), whatever you do, you are not looking after your body as you should. This is totally irresponsible, especially for Christians.

When we were born again we gave our lives to Jesus Christ. All that we are and all that we have belongs to Him. Jesus paid the price for this exchange with the sacrifice of His own life. Therefore, we should honour Him with our bodies.

We have a responsibility to fulfil the reason why we are saved and to do that we need to be fit and healthy.

Personally, I have gone through some major health challenges and, in every situation, the Lord has graciously healed me. I believe that the Lord said to me that He has made me healthy but it is my responsibility to get fit. That is what I intend to do. Well done to the contingent of people who do their best to stay fit but what about you?

Lord Jesus, please help me to honour You with my body. Amen.

7 (A) McKenzie was feeling his age. Do you think that age restricts how we can serve God and why?

7 (B) What does it mean to 'honour God' and how can you honour God with your diet and lifestyle?

7 (C) What will you do this week to honour God with your body? (Read 1 Corinthians 3:16)

8
Beautiful Feet

Isaiah 52:7……How beautiful on the mountains are the feet of those who bring good news, who proclaim peace, who bring good tidings, who proclaim salvation, who say to Zion, "Your God reigns!"

Mountains can be inhospitable, hostile places where people are few and far between. Therefore, when a visitor comes with good news, it is a most welcome sight. The feet that carry the messenger are beautiful!

When the Lord Jesus Christ came over the Mount of Olives, it was to proclaim good news in Jerusalem. The religious leaders were offended and nailed His beautiful feet to a cross on Calvary's hill.

Death couldn't hold Him and, after His resurrection, He ascended back to heaven from the Mount of Olives. When He returns it will be to the Mount of Olives that will split in two when His beautiful feet alight there.

As we climb the mountain of apathy and apostasy it is to bring good news to those who are perishing. We tread in the footsteps of missionaries and martyrs who have gone before us and we do it in the name of Christ Jesus who has made our feet beautiful.

Lord Jesus, help us to walk in Your footsteps. Am

8 (A) McKenzie was walking. To reach some places in the world that is the best way. How far would you walk to take the Good News to others?

8 (B) How well do you know your neighbours and do you ever visit them?

8 (C) What is this 'Good News' that we are meant to carry to others? Challenge yourself to do one thing this week to bring the Good News to someone.

9

Do Not Be Alarmed

Matthew 24:6a……You will hear of wars and rumours of wars, but see to it that you are not alarmed.

The context of this verse is set as a response from Jesus to his disciples' question; *....what will be the sign of your coming and of the end of the age?*

There has never been a time in history when there have been so many wars and rumours of wars. Yet, Jesus tells His disciples, and us, not to be alarmed. As Christians, we can trust completely in God. Jesus, our Lord and Saviour, is with us always. Any fears we may have are dispelled by our faith in God who loves us. Therefore, we are not alarmed.

Looking around us at the awful state of the world, it would be easy to allow what we see to overwhelm us. However, world affairs are not our Lord, Jesus Christ is, and He has overcome the world.

Thank you Jesus, You bring us peace in every situation. Amen

9(A) McKenzie was having a 'daydream'. Does your mind ever drift to past events that trouble you?

(B) The Bible tells us not to worry (Philippians 4:6)? What should you do if you are anxious?

(C) The 'end of the age', 'last days' and 'end times' all refer to the same thing. What does this mean to you and how can you process and talk about these events without being negative and fear-filled?

10

The Lover of Our Soul

Song of Solomon 2:10-12...... My beloved spoke and said to me, "Arise, my darling, my beautiful one, come with me. See! The winter is past; the rains are over and gone. Flowers appear on the earth; the season of singing has come, the cooing of doves is heard in our land.

Song of Solomon is the Bible's love poem. It is an allegory of the love between Jesus Christ and his bride to be, the church.

In *Song of Solomon 2:10-12* we discover that *my beloved* is Jesus and He is speaking to Christians everywhere. This is the time of our courtship. Born again Christian believers are the betrothed bride of Christ.

When we hear his voice there is excitement within us and our hearts beat faster. Jesus is in love with us and He is wooing us.

The *wintertime* of our lives is past; the rainy days are *over and gone*. Now, with Jesus, flowers blossom all around us. We want to sing for joy and nature itself joins with us in jubilant adulation and worship.

Oh, Lord Jesus, thank You for loving us the way You do. Amen.

10 (A) McKenzie was listening. Why is it a good thing to 'listen' to what God has to say to us?

10 (B) What does it means for us to know 'the winter-time and the rains are gone'?

10 (C) Is Jesus your Groom and how can you show Him your love this week?

11
The Lost Sheep

Luke 15:3-6…..Then Jesus told them this parable: "Suppose one of you has a hundred sheep and loses one of them. Doesn't he leave the ninety-nine in the open country and go after the lost sheep until he finds it? And when he finds it, he joyfully puts it on his shoulders and goes home. Then he calls his friends and neighbours together and says, 'Rejoice with me; I have found my lost sheep.'

Metaphorically, Christians are likened to sheep throughout the Bible. Jesus Christ is called, 'the Shepherd'. In the scripture above, one sheep goes missing. Perhaps it wandered away by chance or even deliberately.

The good news is that the shepherd leaves everything and searches for the lost sheep. He finds it, rejoices and throws a party. The point here is that all one hundred sheep belong to the shepherd and when one goes missing he searches high and low until he finds it.

Perhaps you have found yourself separated from the flock. Maybe you have wandered away for whatever reason. Jesus will not give up until He brings you back. He will find you and carry you home.

Lord Jesus, thank You for being the Good Shepherd. Amen

11 (A) McKenzie was searching for a missing person. Have you ever volunteered to help with something and what was it?

11 (B) Every sheep is important to the shepherd; every person is important to God. How does that make you feel about God and have you ever wandered away from Him?

11 (C) Do you know a lost sheep and what will you do this week to help that lost one?

12

Connecting with Jesus

Song of Solomon 1:4……Take me away with you—let us hurry! Let the king bring me into his chambers.

Song of Solomon speaks of intimacy and heart-throbbing passion. The Bride, the Beloved is speaking to her Lover, the King or, in other words, the Christian church is speaking to Christ Jesus.

Are you in love with Jesus? Is Jesus the lover of your soul? Do you long to be locked-in with Jesus in the Most Holy Place, in the inner sanctum of the Holy of Holies?

Song of Solomon, the Bible's racy love poem, describes the passion between two lovers. Are you a beloved disciple? Do you long to get as close to Jesus as possible? Do you long to connect with Him?

Lord Jesus, thank You for waiting for us to connect with You. Amen.

12 (A) Like McKenzie, do you sometimes feel that church worship is 'religious', if so, why?

12 (B) Evaluate your connection with Jesus and how could it be improved?

12 (C) What can you do this week to help someone else with poor connectivity?

13

No Shame

Isaiah 50:7…..Because the Sovereign LORD helps me, I will not be disgraced. Therefore have I set my face like flint, and I know I will not be put to shame.'

No matter what has happened in our past; no matter what we have done or what has been done to us; when we come to know Jesus Christ as our Lord and Saviour, the past has gone and all things have been made new.

The past will not be used to disgrace us or to put us to shame. Man may try to dig up our past, but when we come to Jesus, we become new creations and our lives begin from our Calvary encounter with Christ. We are born again and all our past is washed away by the blood that Jesus shed for us at the Cross.

We can unflinchingly look forward to the great plans that Jesus has for our future knowing, without doubt, that they will come to pass.

Thank You Jesus, my past has gone and I am now a new creation. Amen.

13 (A) McKenzie remembered a verse from the Bible. Learning Bible verses is good for us. Have you memorised any verses and what are they?

13 (B) What are you holding onto from your past and what is hindering you from leaving it at the foot of the Cross? (Read Philippians 3:12-14).

13 (C) As a 'new creation' in Christ who believes in God's forgiveness, what can you change in your behaviour or lifestyle this week to show God that you are trusting Him?

14

Prayer That Words Cannot Express

Romans 8:26......We do not know what we ought to pray for, but the Spirit himself intercedes for us with groans that words cannot express.

As we read this portion of scripture, we discover that there are times when we do not know how to pray as we ought. On those occasions, instead of waiting for the Holy Spirit to lead us into prayer, we often start to pray what we think we should and let loose an eruption of meaningless words that gush out of our mouths, ricochet off the walls and disappear into the air having achieved nothing.

As we continue to speak incessantly with great determination, we build an impregnable wall of words that nothing and no-one can penetrate. We fail to hear God's gentle whisper as He vainly attempts to communicate His will to us.

We are so caught-up in our frenzied barrage that we get lost in a forest of shifting shadows where, sadly, we cannot see the wood for the trees. Skirting around the peripheries of Spirit-led prayer we miss the point. We end up ineffective, frustrated and exhausted.

If we would just stop and wait, if we open up ourselves to hear what the Holy Spirit wants to say, not only will we begin to pray effectively, but He will progressively lead us deeper into prayer *that words cannot express.*

In the deeps with God is where He prays through us; groaning, travailing and interceding. We touch His heart and enter into a phenomenal revelation of His will. It is no longer our words but His, sometimes in our language, sometimes in God's language, sometimes beyond words.

We are caught-up with the Lord in a tremendous place, in the very throne room of God, where His sovereign will for earth is revealed and declared through us, so that His will is done on earth as it is in heaven.

Lord Jesus, thank You for teaching us to pray the way You do. Amen.

14(A) McKenzie was praying in what we call 'tongues'. What do you understand as 'tongues'?

14 (B) Do you find times when you just don't know the words to pray or what to pray for?

14 (C) Take time this week to be quiet before God and ask Him for His words and His prayers. (For clarification you may find it helpful to watch The Way Christians Ministries 'Foundations' course: http://www.globaltfl.com/free-foundations.html)

15

The Fear of the Lord

Proverbs 1:7…. The fear of the LORD is the beginning of knowledge, but fools despise wisdom and discipline.

This scripture does not recommend that we should be afraid of the Lord but rather we should be in awe of Him. We should respect the Lord and at the same time have a healthy dread of displeasing Him. With this attitude we will know Him and do what is right.

This knowledge, once attained, will develop into heavenly wisdom and Christ-like discipline. We would be fools not to pursue and attain such qualities. Heavenly wisdom is the Godly application of the knowledge that comes from knowing God.

Knowing God is having the intimate insights into God that come through our holy reverence and deep love for Him. The wisdom that comes out of this relationship is the manifestation of the character of Christ in us.

What a high and attainable goal. Thank You, Jesus.

15 (A) McKenzie was being held prisoner. Sin can be like a prison. Why?

15 (B) Do you have a healthy fear of God or are you afraid of Him and how can you move from being afraid to awe and reverence

15 (C) Can you love God and still have fears? (Read 1 John 4:18)

16

Every Eye Will See

Revelation 1:7a….. "Look, he is coming with the clouds," and "every eye will see him…"

Jesus Christ is coming back again. Two separate events will take place. Firstly, the Rapture when every believer, both dead and alive, will meet with Christ in the clouds (Read 1 Thessalonians 4:16-17).

Secondly, Jesus is coming back, with us, to reign on earth (Read Revelation 20:4-7).

When He does, every eye will see Him!

With modern technology it will be possible for every eye to see, at the same time, the Second Coming of the Lord Jesus Christ. However, although the event will, no doubt, be televised, God does not need TV to make the world see Him. His Second Coming will be such an awesome event that no-one will miss it wherever they are.

Lord Jesus, come soon. Amen

16 (A) McKenzie was surrounded by modern technology. Does technology have a place in the church today?

16 (B) How would you define 'church' to a non-Christian?

16 (C) What do you think you need to do in order to be ready for the Rapture and what can you change in your life this week in view of that?

17

Lest We Forget

Isaiah 46:9-10 …….. Remember the former things, those of long ago; I am God, and there is no other; I am God, and there is none like me. I make known the end from the beginning, from ancient times, what is still to come. I say: My purpose will stand, and I will do all that I please.

Bill Stone, the last surviving veteran of both World War 1 and World War 2 died, he was 108 years old. I believe that it is of the utmost importance that we remember the men who fought and died for the freedom that we enjoy today. The price they paid was immense; in suffering and in death and in the horrendous conditions they endured on the battlefields.

It is not only veterans of both World Wars that we must remember, there are also soldiers fighting for our freedom in wars today. The weapons of warfare may have changed but the traumatic experiences and devastating carnage remain as atrocious as ever. We must salute and honour those men and women who risk their lives and the many who die each and every day on our behalf.

Of course, there is one war veteran who suffered more than any of us could ever imagine. His name is Jesus Christ, the Son of God.

As He hung on the cross at Calvary, He confronted every demonic power and principality. He took the full weight of the sin of all mankind upon Himself. He was attacked physically, spiritually, psychologically and emotionally, yet He never sinned.

He took our punishment in our place and He won. The battlefield of the cross, where Jesus suffered and died, was the place of our tremendous victory. Jesus overcame sin and death and rose again to secure the greatest victory in the history of the world. The Lord Jesus triumphed on the cross so that anyone who believes in Him will be victorious and live with Him forever.

Let us never forget the war veterans from yesterday and today who paid the highest price for our national freedom, but let us always remember our Lord who gave up everything for our complete and total freedom – Jesus Christ, the saviour of the world.

Thank You Jesus, You have given us absolute freedom. Amen

17 (A) McKenzie was being kept waiting. Patience is a fruit of the Spirit. Can you think of any more? (Read Galatians 5:22-23)

17 (B) Where do we get the strength to fight our battles? (Read Psalm 46)

17 (C) Jesus paid the price for our freedom with His life? How should we respond to this?

18

A Surprise Catch

Luke 5:4…..When he had finished speaking, he said to Simon, "Put out into deep water, and let down the nets for a catch."

After a hard night's fruitless fishing, tired and weary, Simon and his crew returned home. Jesus, to make a space between Himself and the swelling crowd, climbed into Simon's boat. When He had finished, Jesus asked Simon to go back out to deeper water to fish again.

The catch was so huge that their nets began to break. Even after sharing the fish with their partners, the weight of the fish caused their boats to begin to sink. Simon, recognising the power of Jesus, bowed before him in repentance. Jesus told him that from now on he would fish for people.

This graphic story clearly illustrates that obedience to Jesus, regardless of our feelings or our circumstances, will generate miracles for the glory of God.

Lord Jesus, thank You for abundance. Amen.

18 (A) McKenzie was vulnerable and threatened. How do you respond to vulnerability and threats?

18 (B) What would you do if God asks you to do something that doesn't make sense to you?

18 (C) Challenge yourself not to ignore a prompting from God next week, no matter how 'illogical' it may seem.

19

Crisis to Blessings

Psalm 55:23…..But you, O God, will bring down the wicked into the pit of corruption; bloodthirsty and deceitful men will not live out half their days. But as for me, I trust in you.

Trusting in the Lord is a sure path to victory. However, when we find ourselves in a time of crisis our minds can work overtime to look for exit strategies devised from our own understanding.

We pull on the unsanctified resources from our past and begin desperately to dream up schemes that we think may help us. In reality, we are merely leading ourselves into an even bigger mess.

When we deviate from the Lord's plan for our lives we end up in a dead end of destruction. The further into our own plans we go, the closer we move towards unrighteousness and corruption. Stop!

Get back onto the path of righteousness that Jesus prepared in advance for us to walk in. Trust completely in Him and watch how He orchestrates your disaster into triumph and your crisis into blessings.

Lord Jesus, thank You for having the best plan for our lives. Amen.

19 (A) McKenzie hates religion. Can you explain the difference between religion and Christianity?

19 (B) Have you ever deviated from God's path for you?

19 (C) What can you do this week to ensure that you stay on 'the path of righteousness that Jesus prepared in advance for us to walk in'?

20
Get Ready

Malachi 4:5-6 says …. See, I will send the prophet Elijah to you before that great and dreadful day of the LORD comes. He will turn the hearts of the parents to their children, and the hearts of the children to their parents; or else I will come and strike the land with total destruction.

After Malachi, the Old Testament prophet, said these words, there were four hundred years of prophetic silence.

The next occasion when we hear God speak publicly to His people it is from the mouth of John the Baptist in the Gospels. He was preaching a baptism of repentance for the forgiveness of sins.

John came in the spirit and power of Elijah, just as Malachi had said. His ministry was to prepare the way for Jesus Christ's first coming and to get the people ready to receive Him as the Messiah.

However, we learn from the end of Malachi chapter four, and indeed the end of the Old Testament, that this prophecy also relates to the end of the age, *that great and dreadful day of the LORD*. It, therefore, applies both to the first and the second coming of the Lord Jesus Christ. It is a message of revival in these last days.

The message of John the Baptist, like Elijah, was to call the people back to God. That message is, sadly, just as relevant today as it was in the days of Elijah and John.

Thank You, Lord Jesus, for sending messengers to get us ready for Your return. Amen.

20 (A) Maria was angry about what had happened to her as a child. Are there things from your childhood that you have not given to Jesus?

20 (B) How are you getting ready for Christ's return?

20 (C) Do you know Jesus as your Saviour? If not, do you want to? If yes, say this simple prayer. Say it because you mean it with all your heart…..

"I believe that Jesus Christ is the Son of God who came to earth to die for me. I know that I am a selfish sinner. I am sorry for the way I am living and I ask you to forgive me Jesus. With your precious blood shed for me at Calvary's cross, wash me clean of all my sins. I choose to turn away from my sinful ways and ask you, Jesus, to be my Lord and Saviour. Come into my heart and take control of my life. Holy Spirit fill me now and help me to follow Jesus all the days of my life. Amen."

If you have prayed this prayer – congratulations! Tell someone during the coming week.

If you are already saved, is your walk all it should be, if not, how can you make your walk right or better?

21

Boldly Speak the Truth

Isaiah 45:19….I have not spoken in secret, from somewhere in a land of darkness; I have not said to Jacob's descendants, 'Seek me in vain.' I, the LORD, speak the truth; I declare what is right.

As Christians we must endeavour to do what Jesus Christ would do; we should speak the truth and declare what is right. In these decadent days of moral depravity we must speak out against what the world has come to accept as normal.

Gone are honour and respect. Gone too is moral constraint. Forget the evening 'watershed' on TV. Watch the TV before nine o'clock in the evening and you will be sucked into a modern parody of Sodom and Gomorrah.

Have we become desensitised to uncensored promiscuity and sexual deviance? Have our ears stopped hearing the blasphemous swearwords that so readily assault us from our TV sets?

Let's take a stand, a united Christian stand and speak out boldly for the sake of righteousness - for the sake of Jesus. The next time your TV insults you, turn it off! Use the time to send a message to the station to tell them why you turned off. My mind, my heart, my eyes and my ears are not a dustbin for a sick and perverse generation. Are yours?

Lord Jesus, help us to be bold as we speak the truth. Amen

21 (A) McKenzie is working towards ridding the world of nuclear terror. Is there a cause for which you feel passionate?

21 (B) What do you watch on TV and does it glorify God and edify you?

21 (C) What can you choose not to watch and how best might you spend that time during the week ahead?

22

Celebrate Christmas

Matthew 1:23 ……. The virgin will be with child and will give birth to a son, and they will call him Immanuel" — which means, "God with us."

In a world that is desperately searching for answers, we have made a good job of hiding Jesus.

We have successfully removed Him from our western schools and a long time ago we put an 'x' where His name should be in 'Christmas'. There is now a move afoot to remove the traditional festive greeting, "Merry Christmas", from our vocabulary and replace it with "happy holidays".

What about the subtle rise in unsubtly decorating our homes, gardens and Christmas cards with icons of the 'counterfeit trinity'; 'Father' Christmas, the snow-'man' and the 'fairy' lights that shine with electric glory (when they work!)? Please do not misunderstand me, I love Christmas decorations that enhance the joy of the festive season but Jesus not Santa, snowmen, lights and tinsel must remain the real focus of Christmas.

For fear of offending our anti-Christ society we have resorted to tip-toeing around on the eggshells of political correctness. Other faiths are laughing at Christians because they would never dream of making such compromises.

It is time to stand up for Jesus and shout His name from the rooftops. Christmas is all about the Christ.

He is alive, He is here and He is Lord of all; Immanuel – God with us. A child was miraculously born around this time 2000 years ago. In the space of His short life as God incarnate and through His death and resurrection He became the Lord of all.

He conquered sin and death for all mankind and made a way from earth to heaven for those who believe in Him.

If He is your Lord why not let the world know? Let us make these holidays happy for a miserable world by celebrating the birth of Jesus and declaring with one enthusiastic voice, "Merry Christmas".

Powerful and amazing Lord Jesus, You are the Champion of the World at Christmas and all the year round. Amen

22 (A) McKenzie had mixed feelings about Christmas. What do you enjoy most about Christmas and what does Christmas mean to you?

22 (B) A baby is a sign of new life. Why is Jesus' birth so special to us?

22 (C) Some years ago there was a campaign to 'put Christ back into Christmas'. Could you suggest some ways that we could do that?

23

Eternity

Daniel 12:2…..Multitudes who sleep in the dust of the earth will awake: some to everlasting life, others to shame and everlasting contempt.

This scripture speaks of a resurrection of the dead that takes place after the Rapture. The Rapture is the gathering of Christian believers with Jesus in the clouds.

Read in conjunction with Revelation 20 we learn that this resurrection of the dead takes place at the end of Jesus' reign of 1,000 years on earth after His Second Coming.

Those whose name is written in the Book of Life will rise to everlasting life with Jesus but those who have rejected Jesus will be raised to everlasting shame and contempt. They will be separated from God forever.

Mankind was created to be eternal. Death is a temporary state. Where we spend eternity is determined by the choices we make before we die. Where are you going?

Lord Jesus, thank You for calling us to be with You forever. Amen

23 (A) McKenzie had neglected his appearance. Is God concerned about our appearance? Why?

23 (B) We are set apart as Christians. What does that mean for us? e.g. are we to lead isolated lives?

23 (C) Where will (a) those who are separated from God spend eternity and (b) where will you spend eternity? How do you know? (Read Revelation 20). Who can you share with this week that may not be aware of this truth?

24

Live by the Sword - Die by the Sword

Matthew 26:52......"Put your sword back in its place," Jesus said to him, "for all who draw the sword will die by the sword."

The setting is the arrest of Jesus and it takes place just before his crucifixion. John's gospel reveals that it was the disciple Peter who cut off the servant's ear. Jesus heals the servant and his ear is restored. Peter was prepared to fight to save Jesus but Jesus clearly says that this was not the best way in this situation.

Jesus knew that He had come to lay down His life for the salvation of many and, therefore, His crucifixion was inevitable. Jesus did enter into a battle on the cross. It was one of spiritual warfare. He fought against all that Satan could throw at Him and He triumphed over him by the cross. He conquered sin and death for us.

Violence leads to violence but the way of Jesus ultimately leads to lasting joy and peace.

2 Corinthians 10:3-5 says...... *For though we live in the world, we do not wage war as the world does. The weapons we fight with*

are not the weapons of the world. On the contrary, they have divine power to demolish strongholds. We demolish arguments and every pretension that sets itself up against the knowledge of God, and we take captive every thought to make it obedient to Christ.

Lord Jesus, thank You for teaching us how to fight. Amen

24 (A) Miguel was shaken by his ordeal. Has anything ever shaken or shocked you? What was it?

24 (B) How can we live in the world but not be a part of it?

24 (C) Sometimes, we find ourselves in a spiritual battle but, as Christians, we have the victory. What should we do when the enemy attacks us?

25

Actions Speak Louder than Words

1 John 3:18….Dear children, let us not love with words or speech but with actions and in truth.

Love is both a noun and a verb. We do what it says. Platitudes will never be a substitute for passion. Even if we understand what love means, it will always be 'better felt than telt', as we say in Scotland.

However, love is not a masquerade nor is it a charade. Yet, multitudes of people have been horribly deceived by smooth-talking suitors. Sadly, many who sought true love have been short-changed by amorous advances and a fleeting fling.

People in love will go to great lengths to express their love……*For God so loved the world that he gave his one and only Son, that whoever believes in him shall not perish but have eternal life.* (John 3:16). Jesus Christ, God's only Son, willingly laid down His life because He loved us.

How far would you go to demonstrate your love for another?

Lord Jesus, thank You loving us even before we knew You. Amen

25 (A) McKenzie felt sluggish. How can we maintain our 'edge' both physically and spiritually?

25 (B) People remember more of what we do than what we say. How should that effect how we live?

25 (C) Think of someone who needs God's love in their life - what can you do for them next week to show them that love?

26

Unharmed and Untainted

Daniel 3:27......They saw that the fire had not harmed their bodies, nor was a hair of their heads singed; their robes were not scorched, and there was no smell of fire on them.

On the orders of King Nebuchadnezzar, Daniel's three friends, Shadrach, Meshach and Abednego were thrown into the furnace because they would not bow to images of his foreign gods. They proclaimed that their God, Jehovah, would deliver them and, even if He did not deliver them, they would not bow to any other god.

Nebuchadnezzar said, "Look! I see four men walking around in the fire, unbound and unharmed, and the fourth looks like a son of the gods". He ordered them to be released and promoted them saying, "Praise be to the God of Shadrach, Meshach and Abednego, who has sent his angel and rescued his servants! They trusted in him and defied the king's command and were willing to give up their lives rather than serve or worship any god except their own God". Then the king promoted Shadrach, Meshach and Abednego in the province of Babylon.

It is good to know that if we honour our God and do not bow to idols, He will protect us no matter what the circumstances. Not only will he protect us but there will be no taint of worldly things upon us.

When we lay down our lives for Jesus Christ, He delivers us from evil and cleans away the stench of the world we came from. Not only are we set free but his favour is upon us and He will promote us to positions of influence where He places us.

Lord Jesus, thank You for saving and promoting us. Amen

26 (A) McKenzie was waiting to meet Maria. Have you ever made plans that didn't work out?

26 (B) What are the idols in your life and how can you put them aside and honour God instead?

26 (C) What can you do next week to show God He is first in your life?

27

Sin is Sin

Hosea 9:9….They have sunk deep into corruption, as in the days of Gibeah. God will remember their wickedness and punish them for their sins.

The corruption of the people of Gibeah was gross sexual perversion (read Judges chapter 19). We know that in today's society the same corruption exists. Proceeds from the criminal world's ill-gotten gain often finances the sleazy world of pornography. Pornography in turn finances further criminal activities and so on….

However, this verse from the book of Hosea reminds us that God has seen and remembers wickedness and that there is a consequence. The perpetrators of any sin may seem to be very far away from God but it was while we were still sinners that Jesus Christ died on the cross for us.

If sinners die unrepentant in their sinful activities, they will spend eternity in hell. If they repent and give up their wicked ways, God will forgive them. They will be washed clean in the blood of Jesus and be given a completely new life in Christ.

There is no grading of sin. It is not on a sliding scale from one to ten. Sin is sin and it puts a barrier between ourselves and God. Every person on earth is guilty of sin, therefore, we all need to ask for forgiveness to be reconciled to God.

Lord Jesus, thank You for making the way for us to be forgiven. Amen

27 (A) McKenzie looked at the changing face of Glasgow. How has your life changed since becoming a Christian?

27 (B) Do you think some sins really are worse than others and how can you get yourself right with God?

27 (C) Do people see the change in you since you became a Christian?

28

Be Strong and Courageous

Joshua 1:9…..Have I not commanded you? Be strong and courageous. Do not be afraid; do not be discouraged, for the LORD your God will be with you wherever you go.

These words, spoken to Moses' successor Joshua, are also spoken into our lives too. They are not only words to encourage, they are commands. Be strong! Be courageous! Do not be afraid! Do not be discouraged! They are followed by a promise; for I, the Lord of all, your God, will be with you wherever you go! Hallelujah!!

Let this sink in…. No matter where we are, no matter what is going on in and around our lives, our God, Jesus Christ, is the Lord over all our circumstances and situations. He is the Lord.

When we believe this without question, we will be strong and courageous and we will not be afraid or discouraged.

Let's not be bullied by our circumstances. Through what Jesus Christ has done for us at Calvary we have the victory in every area of our lives.

Lord Jesus, You have made us winners. Amen.

28 (A) McKenzie met with people who had no scruples. In life we also may meet such people. How would you react?

28 (B) Paul says in 2 Corinthians 12:10b 'when I am weak, then I am strong.' Why does he mean?

28 (C) Do you know someone you could encourage to be 'bold' and courageous' this week?

29

Free as a Bird

Psalm 124:6-8......Praise be to the LORD, who has not let us be torn by their teeth. We have escaped like a bird from the fowler's snare; the snare has been broken, and we have escaped. Our help is in the name of the LORD, the Maker of heaven and earth.

We can rest-assured that any trap, any snare that the enemy lays for us has been broken by the power of the finished work of Jesus Christ.

In the name of our Lord Jesus Christ, the Maker of heaven and earth, every conniving scheme, every plot to harm us, has been destroyed.

By our faith in Christ Jesus and in the power of His name, we have escaped the devil's clutches. We are free to fly, like the birds of the air, high above every temptation, every snare and every potential danger that comes our way.

Thank You Jesus, You have set us free. Amen

29 (A) McKenzie was alert. How alert are you to things that go on around you?

29 (B) What could hinder you from being free and how can you put aside what hinders you?

29 (C) What does it mean for you that Christ has set you free?

30

Great Confusion

Deuteronomy 7:20, 23.... Do not be terrified by them, for the LORD your God, who is among you, is a great and awesome God..... the LORD your God will deliver them over to you, throwing them into great confusion until they are destroyed.

In this scripture, God Almighty is speaking to the Israelites about how He will defeat their enemies and deliver them into their hands. He tells them that He will confuse and destroy them. Even the enemy leaders will, be handed over to them. He will do this by sending a 'hornet' among them (verse 20).

This same promise still holds true today for the modern Israelites and, indeed, for the land of Israel. As the enemies of Israel gather against them, God Almighty – the same Yesterday, Today and Forever, will supernaturally protect the land and the people.

How can we apply this word to Christians believers in Jesus Christ? Surely, the Lord will confuse those who would mean us harm, those who work through occult powers. The Lord will place forces for good in the midst of them to confuse and destroy them; even their leaders will topple.

The scriptures say that the Lord 'will deliver them over to you'. I believe they will become born again Christians and those they formerly led in the kingdom of darkness they will begin to lead in the Kingdom of Light, the Kingdom of God. Hallelujah!

Lord Jesus, You alone are Almighty God. Amen.

30 (A) McKenzie had to flee quickly from the situation he was in. Do you think he made the right choice and why?

30 (B) Has someone ever tried to harm or hurt you?

30 (C) During this week, choose to pray and forgive your enemies? (Read Matthew 5:44)

31

The Lord Will Satisfy You

Isaiah 58:11....The LORD will guide you always; he will satisfy your needs in a sun-scorched land and will strengthen your frame. You will be like a well-watered garden, like a spring whose waters never fail.

No matter how much of a predicament we find ourselves in, the Lord will guide us out of it and He will give us all that we need to be satisfied. He will strengthen our bodies and cause us to be fruitful.

When we get hot under the collar and stress wants us to blow a gasket.... When we feel burned-out and exhausted, the Lord turns up like a cool stream to refresh us and to bless us. He will never fail us.

Take a breath, hold it....now exhale slowly. The Lord is here and everything is going to be alright.

Mmmmm, thank You Jesus. Amen

31 (A) McKenzie was alone in the Sahara, yet although things were going wrong He was calm. Why is it good to stay calm when things seem to get out of control?

31 (B) Do you ever let the daily events of your life overwhelm you?

31 (C) Do you believe that God is bigger than your circumstances and how can you show that?

32
Love

Song of Songs 8:6-7…..Place me like a seal over your heart, like a seal on your arm; for love is as strong as death, its jealousy unyielding as the grave. It burns like blazing fire, like a mighty flame. Many waters cannot quench love; rivers cannot wash it away. If one were to give all the wealth of his house for love, it would be utterly scorned.

Solomon's description of love in this portion of Song of Songs, places it on a pedestal far above anything else. Love is a strong as death; it is like a blazing fire; it can withstand the power of water and great wealth cannot buy it.

In Solomon's allegorical Song of Songs, Jesus is our Lover and we are His Beloved. Jesus is asking us to place Him, His love, like a seal over our heart and on our arm.

The imagery here is of Jesus being sealed into our heart, His love being sealed-in, and our lives, our arm, belonging to Him so that we choose to walk with Him only. He is jealous of our love and He will not share us with any other. He will be with us always and nothing will make His love for us diminish. We should recognise His love for us as a great treasure that wealth cannot buy.

Lord Jesus, nothing compares to Your love for us. Amen.

32 (A) McKenzie remembered his past as he re-visited his old school. Have you ever re-visited a place from your past that has brought back memories?

32 (B) Is there anything in your life that you love more than Jesus?

32 (C) Read 1 Corinthians 13. Why do you think love is the greatest gift?

33
Always

Matthew 28:20 says……"And surely I am with you always, to the very end of the age."

These words, spoken by Jesus Christ to His eleven remaining disciples, were His parting statement just before His ascension back to heaven. They come at the end of what we now call The Great Commission.

Spoken just before Jesus was taken up into the clouds, these words must have been particularly comforting, if not somewhat confusing. Jesus was referring to an event that would take place ten days after He spoke them. The day of Pentecost would herald the arrival of the Holy Spirit being poured out in fulfilment of what Joel had prophesied (Joel 2:28-31).

Jesus has kept His promise. He is with us today and always, in the power of the Holy Spirit, who comes upon all who believe in Jesus Christ as their Lord and Saviour.

Lord Jesus, thank You for being with us always. Amen.

33 (A) McKenzie had a supernatural encounter with Christ. Have you ever had such an encounter, or dream or vision about Jesus? Can you describe it?

33 (B) Jesus had to ascend back to heaven in order to release the Holy Spirit to come and live within all believers. Do you have Christ, in the power of the Holy Spirit, is living in you?

33 (C) God always keeps His promises. How can you be assured of God's presence in your life?

34
Shout to the Lord

Song of Songs 8:13....You who dwell in the gardens with friends in attendance, let me hear your voice!

Those who love the Lord Jesus Christ have been placed into a well-watered garden; a place of refreshment and blessing. They have been placed there among other believers; friends who help one another.

In an attitude of gratitude for the great things He has done, let us raise our voices together with praise and thanksgiving. Let us raise our voices with shouts of acclamation!

The Lord loves our praises, in fact, He inhabits our praises. When we sing, when we praise God in a loud voice, Jesus is there in the midst of us.

Lord Jesus, thank You for prompting us to raise our voices with thanksgiving. Amen.

34 (A) Although she would have changed, McKenzie still recognised Sarah. What was it that he recognised? Was it her physical appearance or her inner beauty?

34 (B) Do you have an 'attitude of gratitude' and how can you show your gratitude to God?

34 (C) Do you believe you can only praise God at a church meeting? Challenge yourself to spend 15 minutes during your ordinary day (on the bus/in the bath/ in car or train/ at the shops etc, etc…) praising God.

35

What are You Hoping for?

Job 11:18….You will be secure, because there is hope; you will look about you and take your rest in safety.

What are you hoping for? Do you look for it with confidence? If you do, you have faith. Faith comes when God speaks to us. Did God speak to you to believe in what you are hoping for? If not, your hope is no more than wishful thinking!

Can you see, through the eyes of faith, the materialisation of the thing you hope for? Are you sure it will happen as God has said?

Can you rest assured that God's promises are 'yes' and 'amen'? Do you believe that?

Believe and do not doubt, God will give you what you hope for.

Thank You Jesus, those who hope in You are never disappointed. Amen.

35 (A) McKenzie was led to a roadside resting place. Was that by chance or divine intervention?

35 (B) Look at the questions carefully in this chapter and consider them prayerfully.

35 (C) What are you hoping for? Is your hope based on faith or wishful thinking?

36

Fear No Evil

Psalm 23:4.... Even though I walk through the valley of the shadow of death, I will fear no evil, for you are with me....

As Christians, Jesus Christ is our constant companion. For that reason we need not fear anything.

One thing that many people fear is death. For Christians, the death of our bodies on earth means eternal union with Christ.

Even in the shadow of death or in the valley of despair, Christians need not fear anything. Christ Jesus is with us always.

Often when Christians are in life-threatening situations, non-Christians are amazed by our peace and joy. This is our testimony. It is not uncommon for Christians, at the point of death, to sit up with outstretched arms and smile with gratitude and thanksgiving as they are welcomed into the arms of Jesus.

When I was very ill I spent time in a hospital ward for the dying. Most evenings two or three men would die. Those who were non-Christians would cry out with fear and anguish. Those who were Christians were at perfect peace.

Lord Jesus, thank You for being my constant companion. Amen.

36 (A) McKenzie was alive, washed up on the beach. Did God intervene and has God ever saved your life?

36 (B) Do you any fear of dying?

36 (C) Death is not the end, but a new beginning for all eternity. Do you know for certain where you will spend eternity?

37

What Do You Smell?

2 Corinthians 2:16….To the one we are the smell of death; to the other, the fragrance of life.

Not everyone will be happy when we share the Good News of Jesus Christ with them. To some it will speak of death and to others, life.

Those who reject Jesus and His salvation plan will be eternally separated from God. The misconception that death is a long sleep is not true. Death without God is a long, slow, agonising torture forever.

However, those who die with Jesus Christ in their heart will continue to live in God's presence forever. They will not spend any time away from Jesus because as soon as their body dies, their spirit and soul will immediately be with Him.

What do you smell right now? Is it life or death?

Lord Jesus, thank You for calling us into everlasting life with You? Amen.

37 (A) McKenzie noticed a smell. Is your sense of smell important to you?

37 (B) Do smells bring back memories to you, either good or bad?

37 (C) What do you think is meant by 'the fragrance of Christ'?

38

You Did Not Do For Me

Matthew 25:45…….'I tell you the truth, whatever you did not do for one of the least of these, you did not do for me.'

Most Christians are familiar with (and probably prefer) the preceding portion of scripture that looks at the converse, positive scenario.

Jesus is clearly saying that by not helping those who most need help it is like not helping Him. Gulp, what does this mean?

Jesus wants believers in Him to be co-workers with Him. In other words, by helping others as Jesus would we are doing so in His name. When we do this, those we help see the manifestation of Christ in us.

However, by not helping others we miss the opportunity to make Jesus known. We do not make Him manifest and those we could have helped did not see Him. We have failed to magnify the Lord by not helping others. We have failed the Lord.

Jesus came to help the poor and needy and, today, He will work through Christians to do that. If we block His opportunity to manifest Himself in us, we block His opportunity to be all that He is in us. By not doing what Jesus would do to help others, is the same as not doing it for Jesus.

Lord Jesus, please forgive me when I do not help others. Amen

38 (A) Like McKenzie, have you ever stifled something inside – a cry, a scream, something you wanted to say? What was it?

38 (B) What does it mean to do or say something 'in Jesus' Name'?

38 (C) Who do you know who needs help and in what ways can you help someone this week?

39

Do Not Jostle Each Other

Joel 2:7-8….. They charge like warriors; they scale walls like soldiers. They all march in line, not swerving from their course. They do not jostle each other; each marches straight ahead.

What a great image of the church, the body of Christ, Christian believers. Like warriors in attack against the enemy and his plans: scaling walls of opposition and sin; overcoming like soldiers. All in line, of one accord and purpose. No-one swerving or going off on tangents; keeping on course to victory. No-one jostling for supremacy, or trying to be important. Every one of us marching straight ahead, determined to fulfil our destiny, our high calling in Christ Jesus.

Often this is not the way church is, but it could be. Let's declare these words of the prophet Joel over every Christian church. Let's proclaim that this is the way it will be. Hallelujah.

It is God's will to raise up a triumphant and victorious church where the people of God excel, where miracles happen.

These words of Joel show an army of warriors on the move. They are not restricted to buildings. They move powerfully in the world around them overcoming darkness, bringing light, bringing revival in preparation for the Lord's return.

Lord Jesus, we will follow You; the Commander of the Lord's army. Amen

39 (A) McKenzie drew his fighting spirit from the historic roots of his native Scotland. From where do you draw inspiration and strength?

39 (B) Bearing in mind Joel's vision of the church, what do you understand by 'unity'?

39 (C) What can you do next week to serve your church, without expecting recognition?

40

Do Not Let Anyone Look Down On You

1 Timothy 4:12….. Don't let anyone look down on you because you are young, but set an example for the believers in speech, in life, in love, in faith and in purity.

Timothy's mentor, the Apostle Paul, tells him not to allow anyone to under-rate him because he is young. Instead, Paul advises, Timothy is to set a godly example to other believers by his Christ-like lifestyle and character.

Paul's words to Timothy can apply to all of us. There will always be someone who will try to 'pull rank' over us because they have been a Christian for longer. We do not need to prove ourselves to anyone. Instead, by our lifestyle and Christian witness, our actions can speak for us.

Our maturity in Christ is not measured by how old we are or by how long we have been a Christian. Rather, it is measured by how much our lives mirror what Jesus is like.

We do not need to argue out of pride, but instead, submit to those around us out of love and reverence for God. The anointing of the Holy Spirit upon us will make a way for us to shine in all that we do for Jesus.

Lord Jesus, thank You for making me who I am. Amen.

40 (A) McKenzie felt Dale was like a 'diamond'. What qualities make someone a good friend or companion for you?

40 (B) If age bears no relevance to Christian maturity, can older Christians sometimes learn from younger ones?

40 (C) Why is it important not to quench the enthusiasm of younger Christians? Find someone to encourage in your church this week.

41

Made to Succeed

Genesis 14:23……that I will accept nothing belonging to you, not even a thread or the strap of a sandal, so that you will never be able to say, 'I made Abram rich.'

Drive and ambition can be powerful motivators. Attractive offers can be very tempting. However, operating in our own strength outside of a relationship with Jesus Christ, our desire to succeed can grow into a monster that can kill us.

In our own strength we are limited, but in Christ we have unlimited potential in His mighty power. When we hear God's call and respond to His offer of salvation through Jesus Christ, we have access to the awesome creativity that Jesus showed when He made the whole universe.

God wants us to succeed, not only in our short lifespan on earth but forever with Him throughout eternity. He wants us to live our life to the full both now and forever. When we are born again and baptised in the Holy Spirit we will not fail if we follow God's plan for our lives.

Thank You, Lord Jesus, for enabling us to succeed.

41 (A) By accepting Don Pedro's money, Miguel had become entangled with danger. Why is it important that you separate yourself from unrighteousness?

41 (B) Do you want to succeed in whatever you do and to what lengths would you go to try to accomplish that?

41 (C) What is the Christian way to succeed?

42

Hell is a Real Place

Matthew 10:28…… Do not be afraid of those who kill the body but cannot kill the soul. Rather, be afraid of the One who can destroy both soul and body in hell.

Some people say that hell does not exist. Some even say that tough and challenging times on earth are our hell. Both of these comments are wrong. Hell is a very real place. In fact, in the Bible, Jesus talks more about hell that He does about heaven!

Hell is reserved for people who have rejected God's salvation plan through Jesus Christ. They will spend eternity there. However, right up until the moment we take our last breath, we can ask Jesus to forgive us and cleanse us from all unrighteousness, and He will.

Gambling that we can wait to the last minute before receiving Jesus into our hearts is not a wise thing to do. We do not know when our time on earth will be over and death is a master of surprise.

Lord Jesus, please save those who are perishing. Amen

42 (A) McKenzie was given a glimpse of hell. How real is hell to you?

42 (B) What do you believe the Scriptures mean when they talk about hell? (use a bible concordance to look for the words; hell, Hades, Gehenna, Sheol)

42 (C) How can we reveal the reality of hell to others in order for them to choose not to go there?

43

Flawless

Song of Songs 4:6-7……Until the day breaks and the shadows flee, I will go to the mountain of myrrh and to the hill of incense. All beautiful you are, my darling; there is no flaw in you.

King Solomon is writing these words to his lover who will become his wife. It is a love letter. Solomon's writings, under the anointing, have a deeply spiritual meaning also. Therefore, these words spoken by the lover to the beloved represent how Jesus, the Lover of our soul, feels about us, the betrothed church of Christian believers.

The hill of incense metaphorically represents prayer and myrrh is primarily known as an aromatic spice with healing properties. Jesus, now seated 'on high' at the right hand of His Father, intercedes on our behalf day and night. He is our intercessor and our healer.

In the Lord's eyes we are not only beautiful but flawless. The day will come when our Lover will become our husband and, as His bride, we will be made perfect as He is.

Let us rejoice and be glad because the marriage of the unblemished lamb, Jesus, is coming soon. Let us make ourselves ready.

Lord Jesus, thank You for Your immense love for me. Amen.

43 (A) McKenzie was in love. Have you ever been in love, if so, what was it like?

43 (B) Do you believe that to God you are beautiful and flawless?

43 (C) This week, spend some time and write your own private love letter to Jesus (use the next page if necessary).

44

Are You Sitting Comfortably?

Genesis 18:1…. The LORD appeared to Abraham near the great trees of Mamre while he was sitting at the entrance to his tent in the heat of the day.

Abraham was sitting outside his tent, resting in the heat of the day. He was minding his own business when the Lord appeared to him. Abraham was not trying to meet with God, as far as we know, he was resting and the Lord appeared to him.

There is a lesson here for all of us. Sometimes we can try so hard to meet with God that our intensity stresses us out to the point where we are so focussed on our intensions that, ironically, there is no room for God Almighty.

God wants us to substitute our intensity for intimacy. He wants us to relax and meet with Him in our rest. Yes, it's good to have an active spiritual life and a healthy prayer life, you may even fast from time to time, but none of these will make God turn up. We cannot coerce God.

There are a variety of scenarios in which we can meet with God but how amazing is it when He turns up unexpectedly to talk with us and to share His love with us….

Lord Jesus, thank You for appearing in my life. Amen.

44 (A) McKenzie had a 'den' where he could hide himself away. Where do you go to be alone and have privacy?

44 (B) God is a 'God of surprises'. Has God ever surprised you?

44 (C) Do you understand the difference between intensity and intimacy? How do we get intimate with God?

45

Speak Life

John 6:63....The Spirit gives life; the flesh counts for nothing. The words I have spoken to you are spirit and they are life.

Our words have the power to create but they also have the power to destroy. Most people grossly underestimate the inherent power contained in our words.

Jesus Christ fully comprehended the power of His spoken words. His words are Spirit and they are life to all who hear them.

Jesus is the Word of God made flesh and He dwelt among us in a physical form for a brief time two thousand years ago. He still lives among us today in the power of His Spirit, the Holy Spirit. Jesus spoke only the words that His Father taught Him to say. When Jesus speaks, it is God Himself speaking. Therefore, we should listen!

Idle words spoken out of our flesh have no value but they can build up and they can pull down. How many times have we all said something that we regret? With Jesus in our heart as our Lord and Saviour we can speak His words of salvation, healing, encouragement, love and peace.

Lord Jesus, speak Your words from our mouths. Amen

45 (A) McKenzie could hear people talking nearby. Why is it important for us to be aware that people could be listening to what we say?

45 (B) Words, good or evil, come from what is within our heart. What comes from your heart? (Read Luke 6:45)

45 (C) Spend some time thinking prayerfully about your words. Not during your spiritual times but in the office, at school, the supermarket, the train or car. Are they words that build up and encourage others or not?

46

Ask – Seek - Knock

Matthew 7:7-8…. "Ask and it will be given to you; seek and you will find; knock and the door will be opened to you. For everyone who asks receives; he who seeks finds; and to him who knocks, the door will be opened.

Do your prayers get answered or not? Here is a sure way to receive answers to your prayers. It is a simple three stage strategy.

1. **Ask**, but when you ask believe that you will receive what you ask for.
2. **Seek**, but seek until you find what you are looking for. Do not seek half-heartedly, seek with all your heart.
3. **Knock** until the door opens up for you. Be determined and persistent. Do not give up.

Many people pray faithless prayers of wishful thinking. They think that God may or may not answer them. Sadly, because they do not know how to pray effectively, they have hardly ever seen any of their prayers answered. Therefore, they have no faith when they pray. They don't expect a result and that's what they get – no result!

Our prayers, in the first instance, must be inspired by the Holy Spirit of God. He puts into our hearts and into our minds what it is we should pray for.

As we declare and proclaim what we have been given, God uses our words to create His will on earth as it is in heaven. Does that sound familiar? It should, God is the Unchanging One. Why change what works?

Lord Jesus, thank You for teaching us how to pray. Amen.

46 (A) McKenzie climbed a mountain to meet with the terrorists. What mountains do you have to climb in your life?

46 (B) 'Why change what works?'. Do you allow your prayers to be guided and directed by the Holy Spirit and why is it important to do so?

46 (C) Think of something that you have given up praying for and challenge yourself to write down your request and be persistent in prayer on that subject. (Read Luke 18:1-5)

47

A Way That Seems Right

Proverbs 14:12 (NKJV)…..There is a way that seems right to a man, but in the end it leads to death.

Sometimes we can devise all kinds of wonderful plans that stimulate and excite us and maybe even do the same for those around us; but if those plans come from our own understanding and are not inspired by God, they will take us off on a tangent that leads us away from God's plan for our lives.

As Christians we must always commit all that we do to our Lord Jesus Christ. It is crucial that we are busy with what He gives us to do. Otherwise, we can become very busy with what seems to be our 'ministry' but, in fact, is nothing more than our own unsanctified good   ideas.

That path will lead us away from God's plan for our life and, in time, will lead us away from God. Separation from God is spiritual death.

All Christians have been saved for a purpose and God has a desire to see that purpose fulfilled. The enemy would like to see us busy doing all the wrong things. Therefore, it is of paramount importance that we hear clearly from God, with confirmation through His word, to be sure that we are doing what He wants us to do.

Lord Jesus, please help me to follow You on the path You prepared in advance for me to walk in. Amen

47 (A) McKenzie appeared calm but many panicked. How do you behave in times of unexpected crisis?

47 (B) Do you know what God's purpose is for your life, and if so, what is it?

47 (C) How can you know whether you are being obedient to God or just doing a 'good thing' and why is it always good to test any thought or idea we may have against Scripture?

48

Marvellous Light

1 John 1:5......This is the message we have heard from him and declare to you: God is light; in him there is no darkness at all.

God is Light and Jesus Christ is the Light of the World. He has called us out of darkness into His marvellous light. In Him there is no shadow of turning. His light is always at its zenith, always at its peak.

There is no darkness in His light; nothing hidden, nothing obscured.

With God, anything that would lurk in the darkness or hide in the shadows, is exposed. The darkness flees from Him.

In love, His light exposes what is hidden, sometimes even from ourselves. As we bring it into His light it is dealt with and removed. In the light of His presence we are refined and purified.

We are absorbed into His light becoming as He is.

Lord Jesus, thank You for bringing me into Your marvellous light. Amen.

48 (A) McKenzie experienced the 'light of God'. Have you ever experienced the light as McKenzie did and how did it make you feel?

48 (B) Light exposes what is 'hidden'. Is there anything hidden in your life and how can you bring it into the light?

48 (C) How can you be a light in the darkness this week?

Sin is Crouching at Your Door

Genesis 4:7…. If you do what is right, will you not be accepted? But if you do not do what is right, sin is crouching at your door; it desires to have you, but you must rule over it.

This verse creates an image in my mind of sin as a rabid dog, fangs bared in a foaming mouth, waiting at the door of my life ready to pounce and bite me, or anyone else who comes in or goes out of my life.

Once bitten, we are infected by the rabies of sin. We must rule over that dog, master it, so that it does not bite.

Sin is waiting to pounce into our lives through any door of opportunity it can find. We must rule over sin. We have the victory, won for us at Calvary's cross by Christ Jesus our Saviour.

Sin, or a rabid dog, will kill us if it bites. There is an antidote but we must act fast. Get quickly to 1 John 1:9…… *If we confess our sins, he is faithful and just and will forgive us our sins and purify us from all unrighteousness.* Repent of that sin. Jesus will forgive us and cleanse us of all unrighteousness. But don't make a habit of it.

Lord Jesus, thank You for saving us from the consequence of our sins. Amen.

49 (A) McKenzie recognised a potential enemy and dealt with it quickly. Can you discern friends from foes? (Read Ephesians 6:12)

49 (B) Sin 'is crouching at your door'. How can you close that door?

49 (C) Spend some time in prayer and in confessing - read 1 John 1:8-10.

50

Fortified Tower

Proverbs 18:10….. The name of the LORD is a fortified tower; the righteous run to it and are safe.

There is such power and authority in the name of Jesus Christ. Just saying that name can save, heal and set people free.

There is no other name in heaven or earth by which people can be saved. While praying for the sick, simply saying His name is enough to release healing power. Proclaiming His name over the oppressed will deliver them and set them free.

Christians find protection when they call on their Saviour Jesus Christ's name. He can command angels to rescue us in response to our cries. He puts a hedge of protection all around those who believe in Him and in the power of His name. His name is a fortified tower.

In Christ we are safe. He is our refuge; in Him nothing can harm us. We rejoice in our Lord and we praise His name forever.

Lord Jesus, Your name is high and lifted up. Amen

50 (A) McKenzie was always on his guard. Where does your security come from? (Read Ephesians 6:10-18)

50 (B) Proclaiming the name of Jesus can change everything. Do you proclaim His name in every situation?

50 (C) Jesus is our all-in-all. His name is high and lifted up. He will never let us down. Do you believe this? When you have answered, turn the page….

Summary

Now that you have completed this course, please write a short essay to summarise what God has said to you personally. Share your essay with others and please send a copy to me at:

peter@peterstanwaybooks.com

or

Peter Stanway, Kilcreggan House, Argyll Road, Kilcreggan

G84 0JT

UK.

You can write your essay in the blank pages that follow……

(use more paper if necessary)

Essay

Essay

Essay

Global Training For Life

I am hopeful that some readers will progress onto the full online *GlobalTFL course. Currently we are praying that the Lord will raise up 50 Mentors who will oversee 1,000 online GlobalTFL students. Please add your prayers to ours…..

* GlobalTFL link: http://www.globaltfl.com

Amazing Discount

Should you wish to participate in our GlobalTFL course we can offer you a discount from £300.00 (GBP) per semester to only £250.00 (GBP) per semester.

Simply quote this code: 50GBPOFF

Other books by Peter Stanway are available wherever books are sold or from this website:

http://www.peterstanwaybooks.com

COMMENTS

I think it is a great idea to have the course spaced out in fifty weekly episodes and is fantastic bible study material for discussion and sharing. I'm sure it will open up lots of new questions, provide answers and encourage self-seeking. I'm still not in a house group in Singapore, but have a contact to call now and wouldn't it be good to have a McKenzie group out here!

(Carol – Singapore)

I think the idea of putting the two books back to back is a good one. This format will help keep the study portable and easier to refer between the two, whilst only having to carry one book. It will help keep the two parts completely separate but essentially the same entity. It will help feed Christians who are wanting more whilst whetting the appetite of non-Christians, therefore, appealing to both groups. I think it's a clever idea.

(Robbie – Scotland)

I love both the ideas of the covers and of the group study format. I believe designing the covers like that will help identify them as a set but also individual. The group study idea goes right along with the discipleship you already conduct, so this would be a natural progression and a much needed one, in my opinion. To be able to offer it worldwide is a benefit to everyone.

(Mary – USA)

Oh, one other thing. It's the best writing about Song of Songs since Hudson Taylor's brilliant book on the subject... you could do a book on that as a stand-alone, cheers.

(Katharine – Australia)

Who is McKenzie?

On its own, *Who is McKenzie?* is a terrific outreach tool to give as a gift to your unsaved family and friends. It is a non-religious, de-jargonised glimpse into the adventures of McKenzie. We travel the globe and enter into the fascinating world of McKenzie. In an intriguing and breath-taking diversity of adventures McKenzie, goes through a plethora of spiritual and emotional experiences. We question what will happen to McKenzie while facing the same life-changing questions that we ourselves must answer......Everyone will identify in some way with the central character, but just who is McKenzie?

www.PeterStanwayBooks.com

This book is also available wherever and however books are sold

ISBN 0-9839186-4-3

ISBN13 978-0-9839186-4-6

ALSO AVAILABLE FROM PETER STANWAY

Wee Boys from Glasgow Don't Cry

An autobiographical real life story of personal transformation

Wee Boys from Glasgow Don't Cry is a challenging real-life roller-coaster story of survival and victory. In the twilight zone of drugs and alcohol, Peter spirals deeper into a desperate lifestyle with no holds barred. On the run with another man's wife, extreme personal transformation is just about to hit him! Completely dysfunctional from years of hedonism he is thrown a lifeline from where he last expected. With no options left, Peter grabs the outstretched hand of Jesus. The power of God knocks him to the floor. When he gets up he is totally changed. The real adventure is about to begin …..

Buy from www.PeterStanwayBooks.com

This book is also available wherever and however books are sold

ISBN-100-9772194-4-5

ISBN-139780977219445

world slamming their spiritual fist on a table demanding to know the truth. I know because I was one of them. I grew up in church but failed to know, really know, God. It is my prayer that as you read Who Is McKenzie?, your eyes will be opened, the truth revealed, and for the impact of that truth to reach forward into generations to come. Whether you need to wipe your slate clean as I did, or to hear the message for the first time, I believe Peter will profoundly affect the way you view God. For those that want to know Him and bypass the doctrinal sludge that tends to weigh us down, McKenzie is perfect.' Mary Nichelson Editor, journalist, talk show host – USA

CONTACT DETAILS

http://www.peterstanwaybooks.com

Comments

'Pure Genius!' Robert Bruce Chief Petty Officer Royal Navy Submariner - Scotland

'Am I McKenzie?' Pamela Taylor Beauty Therapist - Scotland

'The vision of Jesus is brilliant, praying in tongues brilliant and I loved the chapter about McKenzie's den in Kenya.' Katharine Baumanis palliative care nurse – Australia

'Excellent! I thoroughly enjoyed it all. Vivid descriptions and memorable locations from all around the globe.' Thomas Thomson Student - Scotland

'McKenzie is profound! I am moved to tears at several points, not because the action is emotional, but rather the content and questions and his wonderings resound in all of us. This is from God, I am so sure of it. For those that want to know Him and bypass the doctrinal sludge that tends to weigh us down, McKenzie is perfect.

Several years ago, a military drama premiered on silver screens across the world in which one line has become notorious for making the movie. In the famous courtroom scene, a lawyer slams his fist on the table while yelling at the defendant, "I want the truth." In much the same way, I see believers around the

Prayer

Well done, you have reached the end of *Who is McKenzie?*. I hope that you enjoyed it. Perhaps, like McKenzie, you have had many experiences in life and you have questions about deeper spiritual truths. Some of the answers to your questions will not come from your intellect they will come from revelation by the Spirit of God. Maybe you already know this.

If you truly want to know God personally for yourself, you first need to ask Jesus Christ into your life. If you are ready to do this, please say this short prayer. You can use your own words if you prefer….. *"I believe that Jesus Christ is the Son of God who came to earth to die for me. I know that I am a selfish sinner. I am sorry for the way I am living and I ask you to forgive me Jesus. With your precious blood shed for me at Calvary's cross, wash me clean of all my sins. I choose to turn away from my sinful ways and ask you, Jesus, to be my Lord and Saviour. Come into my heart and take control of my life. Holy Spirit fill me now and help me to follow Jesus all the days of my life. Amen."*

If you have prayed this prayer – congratulations! Tell someone as soon as you can and find other Christians who will help you to grow in your faith. I would love to know too. You can send me an email: peter@peterstanwaybooks.com or write to: Peter Stanway, Kilcreggan House, Argyll Road, Kilcreggan G84 0JT UK

The poker in his assailant's hand bounced off the hall carpet. Mr Jeffrey staggered backwards dazed and with a bleeding nose. Poor old Mr Jeffery, McKenzie's kind-hearted next-door-neighbour. Believing the house was empty, he was suspicious when he saw the light on in McKenzie's study. That would teach him to stick his (now bleeding) nose into someone else's business.

No real harm was done and soon the neighbour's were best friends again. They had a good laugh at their own, somewhat pathetic, attempt at heroics, slowly shaking their heads like two nodding dogs on the parcel shelf of a family car. They smiled as they reminisced over a cup of tea. 'There had been a time…. and it seemed like only yesterday', mused Mr Jeffrey. McKenzie, now far away in another place with his own thoughts, said nothing….

50

McKenzie and the Toilet Brush

McKenzie stretched himself like an old dog getting up after a long sleep in front of an open fire. His bones cracked but it felt good. McKenzie had been sat in front of his PC for far too long. He took a big drink of his cool*ish* diet coke, burped, broke wind and went to the toilet. He thought he was in the flat on his own but he wasn't….

Through the space under the toilet door McKenzie was sure that he saw a shadow moving; no sound but a shift of light. He was convinced that someone was waiting to attack him outside the door.

McKenzie looked around for something that he could use as a weapon. All he could see was a toilet brush. It was fairly sharp at the end of the handle but it would be no use against a gun or a knife.

Quietly, he pulled up his trousers and remembered not to flush the toilet thus signalling his imminent exit. Fortunately, the door opened outward and McKenzie pushed it open as fast and as hard as he could. His assailant was behind the door and, much to McKenzie's satisfaction, it thumped hard against him.

turf. McKenzie flipped open his secure mobile phone and made a call to Captain Stein of Homeland Security….

49

McKenzie and the Unscheduled Stop Over

Due to the quiet two-o'clock-in-the-morning roads, the bus that took the disgruntled passengers from Cincinnati Airport to the hotel (courtesy of Delta Airlines) made good and comfortable progress on the twenty miles journey. There were only fifteen people who had to sleep-over on account that there was no late night flight from Cincinnati to Detroit.

Bleary-eyed but resigned to the necessity of the unscheduled stop-over, McKenzie casually perused his fellow passengers. His eyes stopped to take a second look at a certain Asian passenger. McKenzie couldn't be certain but he thought he recognised him from a recent visit he had made to Northern Pakistan. Surely not, it couldn't be?

Once in his room, McKenzie typed-in his password and activated the fingerprint recognition on his laptop. He opened up the encrypted file containing details of his recent trip to Pakistan and, there he was, Ashar Abdul Sohail.

Asher had been flagged-up as someone to watch as a potential threat to the delicate balance of power between the insurgent terrorists and the western allies who, at any cost, would do everything possible to prevent terrorist activities on their home

Peace began to soak him like mist on a mountainside; like a breath. A gentle breeze caressed him in love. McKenzie didn't want it to stop. He thought that his heart would burst with such tremendous elation, a symphony of love, joy and peace. Still it came, wave after wave of enrapturing harmony.

McKenzie felt at one with all that was happening. He blended into the light and the love until he was completely unaware of himself. He knew that he had been saved from utter, unending evil and he was now soaked and saturated in this expansive, great goodness. He didn't want it to stop and somehow, deep inside, he knew it never would…..

48

McKenzie in the Light

The smell of sulphur and the stench of filth made McKenzie want to retch. It overpowered him; dank, putrid decay, the reek of death. The tortured screaming was at fever-pitch way beyond the capabilities of anything human.

Involuntarily, McKenzie let out a scream himself. It came from somewhere deep within and inside that desperate cry was every ounce of McKenzie's last hope of survival.

Out of nowhere McKenzie suddenly felt his fall being cushioned by an invisible source. Instead of falling downwards into the jaws of the devouring black evil abyss he was travelling upwards at the speed of light towards a glorious, magnificent, iridescent interweave of brilliant colours. McKenzie was exhilarated, he was overwhelmed with euphoria. Elated and filled with tremendous joy, McKenzie lay back into the invisible arms and enjoyed the ride.

All of a sudden, McKenzie was in the centre of an inexpressible light. Colours flashed all around him. He could almost touch and taste each colour. However, as he reached out to take hold of them they morphed into yet another holographic display of tremendous beauty.

47

McKenzie is Diverted

As McKenzie carefully made his way back to his seat from the toilet, he was aware that the sleeping passengers with upturned, open-mouthed faces didn't notice that the turbulence was getting stronger. McKenzie was almost thrown into his seat. The 'fasten seatbelts' sign lit up and the cabin crew announced that it was necessary for all passengers to return to their seats to ride out the storm. Lightning flashed outside the window. It lit up the heavy rain and the angry black clouds.....then another flash.

This time McKenzie saw the fork lightning hit the wing of the plane. The reassuring voice of the pilot calmly told everyone onboard the 737 that one of the starboard engines had been 'immobilised' by the storm and the plane was being forced to make an emergency landing at the next airport, Cincinnati.

A wave of panic broke over every passenger who was awake, incredulously some continued to sleep completely undisturbed by the raging storm and potential danger.

Cincinnati was not where McKenzie was heading. His contact in Detroit would have to wait until his next connecting flight.....

wanted status and a land and a nation of their own. How this could ever be given was impossible to imagine. Al-Qaeda, also known as the International Islamic Front for Jihad against the Crusaders and the Jews, made their fight with everyone who is not on their side.

McKenzie's main task was to dissuade them from using their WMD. Getting them to lay them down would require a miracle. The ultimate aim of al-Qaeda is to destroy America by bringing about its economic collapse. They aim to do this by goading them into a 'War on Terror' in a variety of Muslim countries. In doing so, al-Qaeda hopes to drain the USA economy.

The strain of multiple engagements in numerous places would make the worldwide economic system, dependant on the USA dollar, also collapse and that would lead to global political instability. In turn, this will ultimately lead to a worldwide jihad led by Al-Qaeda. Their ideal, after that, would be to establish an ultra conservative form of Islamic government to rule across the world.

If ever McKenzie needed to pray, it was now....

46

McKenzie in the Mountains

Ensconced in the Himalayas of Northern Pakistan, McKenzie, in a vain attempt to cut out the draughts and beat back the deadly cold, wrapped himself tightly in the inadequate blanket he had been given.

He was in this bombed-out hell hole to meet the al-Qaeda leaders who had wreaked havoc on the unsuspecting infidels of the west. Hiding out in a network of underground caves, this little group of terrorist extremists had masterminded the worst Machiavellian acts of evil since the Gestapo of the Second World War.

McKenzie had managed to secure a meeting with them only days before their planned attack on the city of London. He hoped to dissuade them from 'pressing the button' with offers of power and influence within the Pakistani government. Oh yes, this they already had albeit illegally, but McKenzie hoped that the offer of recognised status from many of the World Powers would sway them.

They treated McKenzie with respect, they knew who he was but McKenzie would have to offer them a lot more than recognition. The Al-Qaeda leaders had set their sights high, they

45

McKenzie and the Yacht Club

As McKenzie waited for Miguel to show, he nursed an iced diet coke and allowed his eyes to drift over the bobbing boats moored in front of him; big yachts, cabin cruisers, modest boats for sale and ostentatious beauties that would cost millions of Euros.

Overly loud laughter and cockney accents caught his attention. McKenzie couldn't make out their words but he could pick up the brash vibe of Costa criminals revelling in exaggerated stories from their shared past.

McKenzie knew from experience that they weren't swapping stories of recent criminal activities. They would more likely be sharing anecdotes of past exploits and prison sentences, having a laugh at triumphs and failures involving the criminal fraternity that they all knew.

This wouldn't be loose talk, no, careless talk cost lives and that life could be yours! McKenzie knew that this strip of coastline from Torremolinos to Marbella was a favoured hide-out for foreign criminals and a hallowed haven for cooling off after a big job.

McKenzie felt uncomfortable just being within earshot. He hoped Miguel would show soon…..

Ogembo was a market town where most of the surrounding farmers sold their produce. It was close to the equator and it rained a lot giving it a warm, tropical climate. The land was fertile producing mostly white maize and tea.

McKenzie loved to live like a native when he was in Ogembo. However, he kept himself to himself, preferring solitude to socializing. He knew the locals and they knew him. He thought he knew their primitive ways until, one day unannounced, a stranger turned up……

44

McKenzie Builds a Den

As a child, McKenzie loved his hiding places or 'dens' as he called them: a Scottish word presumably derived from the word 'hidden'. He could climb into his den, into his imaginary world, and be lost in wonder for days.

As an adult, McKenzie still loved to hide away from time to time. He had a network of dens all over the world. He had one deep in the Amazonian Rain Forest of Brazil and he had another in Ogembo, a town of little consequence in Western Kenya.

When he was a child, around the age of six, McKenzie had lived in Kisumu, in a military compound, with his parents. Ever since then he had a soft spot in his heart, filled with happy memories, of the people and the place.

His boyhood friend Blessing's grandfather had died, leaving his house in the countryside of Ogembo, empty. The distance from Kisumu to Ogembo was a little over eighty miles, so McKenzie bought it. It was a *Nyamwezi*, a circular building with walls made of mud and cattle dung. It had one solitary low door, a little window and a thatched roof. It wasn't much to look at but it was McKenzie's Kenyan den.

43

McKenzie Fans the Flame

It had been three days since the school reunion. McKenzie had hardly slept a wink. Every time he thought about Sarah, his heart skipped a beat. She had readily agreed to meet McKenzie for coffee in a city centre café in the heart of the, now fashionable, Merchant City area of Glasgow.

McKenzie had discovered that Sarah had been widowed by a freak accident that caused her husband's single-engine light aircraft to crash, killing him instantly. That was seven years ago.

Sarah had raised Maggie single-handedly while working as a research scientist in the labs attached to Strathclyde University. Maggie, having just finished her exams, was about to become a student at Strathclyde Uni where she hoped to study and to follow in her mother's footsteps.

McKenzie felt like a young boy again, besotted and head-over-heels in love. He wanted, above all things, to wrap his arms around Sarah and squeeze her close to himself. He wanted to kiss her luscious red lips, but he would have to wait.

Firstly, he had to find out how Sarah felt about him....

42

McKenzie Plunges into Darkness

McKenzie was spiralling backwards, falling into empty darkness. He felt helpless; unable to coordinate his movements; unable to think straight. What was happening to him? He had no idea.

He reached out desperately, trying to catch hold of something, anything to stop him falling. He grabbed at something horrible and slimy that gave him the creeps but it slipped from his grasp.

As it slipped from his grasp, McKenzie saw the ugliest face of indescribable evil stare back at him. It had piercing dark eyes that gripped his soul. Panicking, McKenzie scanned the unyielding void. At that moment the screaming started: eerie, spine-chilling, blood-curdling screaming, first one demented, twisted voice then another and another.

The cacophony was overwhelming; ear-splitting, unrelenting like slow sadistic torture to the point of death but death, like a predator, toyed with its prey.

Spinning, spiralling deeper, McKenzie plummeted downwards into the gaping jaws of whatever awaited him in the chasm below.....

McKenzie made his way there, thinking it should be quiet at this time of the day……

41

McKenzie Finds Some Shade

Even on the promenade, *el paseo maritimo*, in Fuengirola, there was hardly a breath of air. Not even a sea breeze. McKenzie sat on a bench under the sparse shade of a sapling orange tree.

He marvelled at the hoards of foreign holiday makers laid out on towels along the beach like meat on a barbeque griddle. They turned themselves over to get thoroughly cooked. Their skin tones ranged from raw pink to well done.

It was two o'clock in the afternoon and McKenzie remembered that only mad dogs and Englishmen went out in the mid-day sun. He was here to meet Miguel, the fisherman who had worked in *La Carihuela* at the time when he pulled up in his nets what was left of Don Pedro's ex-Columbian overseer, Paco. That was a while ago.

Don Pedro had sent Miguel a gift that he couldn't refuse. He told him to keep the details of his surprise catch suitably vague. With that money Miguel had bought a bigger fishing boat and he now sailed out of Fuengirola's fishing port. McKenzie had arranged to meet Miguel in one of the expensive yacht club bars at the other side of the port.

40

McKenzie Finds a Diamond

McKenzie found a diamond, and a rough diamond at that. Dale was precious and he didn't even know it. With a little spit and polish he could become a very valuable asset to McKenzie's mission.

Dale was smart, but he was also innocent, almost to the point of being naïve. He could learn all that McKenzie had to teach him. On top of all that, McKenzie liked him even if he was a little quirky.

He would invite Dale to accompany him on a couple of trips and he would teach him by example. McKenzie was excited; he could sure use help and Dale was it! Just lately McKenzie had felt exhausted; worn-out and frazzled. Young blood, that's what he needed.

Mexico was already on McKenzie's radar, Dale would love it and McKenzie felt sure he would rise to the challenge…..

They had usurped the power of the Pakistani government and used them as a façade to hide behind. They had gained control of the Pakistani defence systems and al-Qaeda now had full nuclear capability.

McKenzie knew exactly what was going on, he drew his intel from the darkest inside sources. Al-Qaeda intended to fire a nuclear bomb and the target was London. This news hadn't hit the media yet and that gave McKenzie a small window of opportunity before the panic started.....

39

McKenzie the Warrior

To McKenzie they looked like giant claymore-wielding warriors; to others they were wind turbines that revolved majestically in lines across the undulating hills of the Southern Uplands of Scotland.

In a bygone era, ferocious warriors would have lined these same hills; tartan-clad armies that fought face-to-face with every invader. The Scots were fearless, even wild, and they were feared by every adversary who came against them. Throughout history, from the Picts until now, Scottish soldiers were infamous in battle.

McKenzie had a fighting spirit, a warrior spirit. He was as tenacious as a West Highland Terrier and he was a champion of his cause to oppose the use of nuclear terrorism. He was respected by both good and bad alike.

Now was the time to pull from his Scottish DNA, to summon every ounce of courage he could muster. The al-Qaeda Jihadists had progressively infiltrated Pakistan from the north. They had caused carnage among the tribal factions and, through a carefully planned strategy of bombings and kidnappings, they had brought fear and terror among the placid Pakistanis.

passionate about doing all that he could to help them. He was on the Board of Directors of some large charities but it was the little, less well known NGO's, that he really wanted to help most. Those that weren't afraid to get their hands dirty, those that moved in close-up-and-personal and got in among the people they wanted to help.

Today, he was flying the flag for *'Make a Change'*, a little-known feeding charity that provided meals for school age children in the world's poorest places. McKenzie wanted to do all he could to help them. He waited his turn to speak and when he did, he shot from the hip. Money, not manners, were what was needed most....people were dying because of political correctness. It was time for action, now!

38

McKenzie Tames a Scream

McKenzie felt decidedly uncomfortable. He was twitchy and he was agitated. A quiet scream began to form deep inside him. He had to get out of there, now!

A combination of last night's over-indulgence and the droning monotone of a serious contender for the world's most unmotivational speaker gave McKenzie an insatiable desire to escape.

Boardrooms were among McKenzie's least favourite places to be. The complex interweave of personalities, megalomaniac egos and secret agendas filled the room like the stench from an open sewer.

The scream within him was about to burst out, but McKenzie had to tame it and remain silent. It was for the greater good of the cause. How else was he ever going to see a difference made to the plight of the untold multitudes of abandoned, marginalised and forsaken people who were lost in a savage world that was not their own?

McKenzie was moved with such deep compassion at the condition of those less fortunate than himself. He was absolutely smell of eau de toilette. Blessing's mother must have splashed it on her children to keep them smelling fresh in the hot African sunshine.

*   *   *

As soon as the family sat next to him on the plane he smelled it: that same clean, fresh smell. They must have been rushing to catch their flight; a mother, her two children and, McKenzie presumed, a family friend. He breathed deep and enjoyed the memories that the smell evoked…..

37
McKenzie and the Smell

It was the smell that first caught McKenzie's attention. It transported him back to a time when he lived in Kisumu, Kenya. He was six years old.

*   *   *

McKenzie's family lived in the security of the military compound where his father had been unexpectedly stationed. McKenzie made friends quickly with some of the other white children, but it was the Kenyan children that he liked the most. He had never known any black kids before.

Blessing was a boy roughly the same age as McKenzie, but that's where the similarities stopped. Blessing had a younger sister called Precious. Together they came into the compound every day. While their mother cleaned around the houses her children would sit, well behaved, on the carefully tended lawn.

When it came time to clean McKenzie's family home, McKenzie would go out to play. Blessing loved football and so too did McKenzie. They didn't speak each other's language but football knew no language barriers. During the rough and tumble of close-contact hot and sweaty games, McKenzie noticed the fresh very much on edge and his mind was working overtime as he desperately tried to hatch a plan for escape.

The sound of a racing engine distracted him. He looked into the distance and saw a small, white speedboat racing towards Don Pedro's opulent cruiser. There was a sudden moment of panic interrupted by an almighty explosion as the speedboat slammed into the side of 'La Dama de la Noche'.

'It must have been crammed full of explosives', thought McKenzie just before everything went dark…..

36
McKenzie is Shipwrecked

McKenzie slowly regained consciousness. He was lying face down in the sand. When he tried to move, every part of his body ached. What had happened, how did he get here?

His mind went back to the speedboat making directly for 'La Dama de la Noche', Don Pedro's luxury yacht. Don Pedro's men had caught up with McKenzie in Gibraltar where he had been attending a top-level, highly secretive meeting with military brass deep in the hollows of the Rock. When he stepped out of the black, chauffeured, diplomat's limo onto the steps of his hotel, Don Pedro's thugs had jumped him.

Hooded, bound and gagged, McKenzie was taken to 'La Dama de la Noche' where he was drugged and dumped below decks. After who knows how long and still fuzzy from the after-effects of the drugs, Don Pedro summoned McKenzie, unbound, to the fishing deck upstairs. While McKenzie had been unconscious below decks the yacht had left the marina and was now far out in open waters.

In an exaggeratedly benevolent voice, Don Pedro took delight in recounting the graphic details of how Maria had died: every gory detail. Now it was McKenzie's turn to die. McKenzie was

35

McKenzie Finds Hope

McKenzie scanned the parched desert landscape expecting to see nothing, but hoping that he would see something or someone, some kind of life, anything. As his trained eyes journeyed slowly through the bleak, arid, inhospitable terrain, he stopped to look again at a speck in the distance. It hovered in the shimmering heat. It may have been his imagination, it may have been a mirage, but it was worth checking out.

McKenzie filled up his canteen with water from the drum in his pick-up and set off in the direction of that indistinguishable fragment of hope. As he got closer the speck grew larger and took on a distinct shape. When he finally reached it, McKenzie discovered with delight that he had stumbled upon a caravanserai: a roadside resting place where travellers could relax and recover from the day's journey. These caravanserai supported the flow, albeit sporadic, of commerce, information, and people across the network of trade routes throughout North Africa.

Although currently deserted, McKenzie knew that, eventually, some desert nomads or, perhaps, a travelling trader, would stop by for refreshment. All he had to do was wait…..

Like a body blow from a prize fighter, the shock of instant recognition took his breath away. It was her, it was Sarah. Amazingly beautiful, her perfect teeth flashed pearly white behind her warm, charismatic smile. She was engaged in animated conversation with a group of young adults. One of them, who was both pretty and elegant, caught McKenzie's eye and came striding over to him.

'Dr McLeod', she said respectfully, 'I had the honour of being at your talk to the school two weeks ago. It was marvellous. Please, I would love to introduce you to my friends'. Before he had time to think, McKenzie was being chaperoned across the room into the midst of the group he had been studying. 'These are my friends; Toby, Libby, Tom, Shelly and I'm Maggie. This is my mother.'

'Sarah', blurted McKenzie.

'Why, McKenzie!' smiled Sarah, 'where have you been hiding?'.....

34

McKenzie Meets His First Love

When he had finished speaking at Glasgow Academy, over a cup of tea the Headmaster thanked McKenzie personally, and in the course of polite conversation happened to mention that the Annual Pupil's Reunion was about to take place in two week's time.

Trying not to appear too interested, McKenzie made a mental note of the details and began to let his mind wander. It was a long shot, a very long shot. Sarah Stewart could be anywhere with any one, not to mention children….

The day came and McKenzie decided to dress 'smart but casual'. As he dressed he couldn't help notice how nervous he was. 'Take a deep breath,' he told himself, 'relax'. This was ridiculous. The palms of his hands were sweating.

He helped himself to a courtesy drink when he entered and began to scrutinise the people who were gathering. What was he looking for? Sarah would probably have changed beyond all recognition. His eyes slowly roamed around the room stopping briefly at anyone who loosely fitted how she had looked twenty-five years ago.

that carried him off into the most peaceful sleep he had ever known.

Instantly McKenzie felt his heart melt and absolute trust mixed with tremendous gratitude gushed out of his innermost being. He had never felt such love for anyone or anything. McKenzie was transfixed.

'I am with you always'.

McKenzie believed it! He watched his friend's powerful arms open outwards. A kaleidoscope of colours spilled over McKenzie's upturned face. He knew that his new companion loved him enough to die for him. His heart beat so strongly that McKenzie thought it would burst. As he stared open-mouthed, his new best friend began to evaporate into an ethereal mist and disappear into the atmosphere that was pregnant with his presence.

McKenzie continued to stare into the empty space that had been temporally filled by the most glorious being he had ever seen. His mind could make no sense of it, but inside – deep inside, he knew he need never fear anything ever again. The sound of silence enveloped him as he slowly lay back down, his heart was still thumping inside his chest.

'Thank you', he said out loud to his friend. McKenzie was so overwhelmed he thought he would explode with joy.

'Thank you, McKenzie,' came the response, like a gentle whisper

33
McKenzie has an Encounter

McKenzie sat bolt upright, his eyes popping. He was now completely awake but his 'dream' continued in vivid colour. There, in front of him, was a man, an incredibly handsome man, who seemed to emanate a brilliant bright light. His shoulder length hair was illuminated making it look like there was a halo around his head.

The light, although powerful, was not glary. It had a translucent effect that shimmered like a gossamer haze revealing the full spectrum of a magnificent rainbow arching around his unexpected visitor.

McKenzie felt elated, overwhelmed with joy. His guest's face shone with a broad friendly smile full of perfect white teeth. His eyes creased with laughter-lines.

'Peace be with you', he said, with a voice that sounded like a waterfall.

A wash of peace, unlike anything McKenzie had ever felt, flooded over him.

'I am your friend', he continued with the same beautiful voice.

The sound of his name jolted McKenzie back to the present. He was introduced to the school as 'the leading expert in the clandestine world of secret weapons'. He waited for the applause to subside before he began…..

32

McKenzie Goes Back to School

One day, out of the blue, a letter arrived inviting McKenzie to speak at his old school in Glasgow. They wanted him to speak about, 'The Secret Weapons of Mass Destruction'.

McKenzie had not been back to Glasgow Academy since he left in 1986. Memories came flooding back as soon as he entered the School Assembly Hall where he was to address the entire school, pupils and staff. McKenzie felt honoured.

Events that he had long forgotten returned with High Definition clarity. When he stood to the side of the podium waiting to be introduced, his eyes scanned the immaculately uniformed audience. There were more than thirteen-hundred pupils present.

McKenzie's mind flashed back to his third year at the school and to his first serious crush on the very beautiful Sarah Stewart. She was as brilliantly academic as she was stunningly gorgeous. She had wavy raven-black hair that flowed over her shoulders and halfway down her back, her eyes were deep hazel pools of mystery and her flawless olive skin faultlessly complemented her petite and perfectly defined figure....

Stay calm, McKenzie told himself, there *is* a solution…..

31

McKenzie Gets Cooked

The wind died away leaving McKenzie sitting in the merciless inferno of airless sunshine. He felt like an experiment on oxygen deprivation. He focussed his mind and tried to find a place inside his head where he could cope. He tried not to sweat but beads of perspiration began to form on his forehead and he felt trickles of sweat run down his rib cage. There was nowhere to hide.

McKenzie's car, like McKenzie himself, had overheated on the sand-covered single-track road that ran from Reganne to In Salah through the Algerian Sahara. Wisely, he had a five-gallon drum of water in the back of his borrowed pick-up. McKenzie had turned off the engine to allow it to cool down. As he waited his mind went back to Spain and to Maria. She knew nothing of his whereabouts and, therefore, no amount of torture would make her give him away. He hoped that she would not suffer long before she died.

Vultures circled high overhead but McKenzie was determined that he was not going to become a carrion feast for them to gorge on. He popped the bonnet; there was a gentle hiss of steam as he opened the radiator cap. Bracing himself on the front bumper, he carefully began pouring water into the radiator. Immediately, it ran straight through, soaking his feet. The radiator was blown.

What would happen to the big weapons, the really big ones, the existing nuclear missiles or the ability to build them? McKenzie would need to tune into the jungle drums, to eavesdrop on who was talking and to whom……

Later, from a safe haven in Paris, he had time to think. McKenzie was looking for answers. The biggest shift of global power since the fall of the Roman Empire had taken place suddenly. The stage was set, the demography of WMD was about to change forever.

What now? questioned McKenzie. In a very short space of time, the politics and balance of power in the Arab countries of North Africa and the Middle East had been revolutionised. Tyrannical dictators and corrupt governments had been replaced by rebel leaders who promised 'a time of change' for the good of the people. Where had he heard that before?

It all sounded like a hollow echo that had originated from the west. The prospect of these oil rich countries being governed by inexperienced young people, still high from their adrenalin-rush, sent warning signals to McKenzie. He sensed danger. Who would pull the strings?

The 'super powers', in fact, most countries around the world, recognised the authority of the victorious revolutionaries. However, would the new leaders be manipulated by outside powers eager to ally or, equally sinister, by hidden radicals from within....?

30

McKenzie in the Cross-Fire

McKenzie never thought for a moment when he went to Tunisia that all hell would break loose. He had arranged to meet Aziz in Beni Khiar, a small town on the peripheries of the tourist trail that leads to Hammamet and not too far from the cosmopolitan city of Nabeul. It had seemed like a good idea to McKenzie to build in some rest and relaxation while he went about his business, under cover, as a tourist.

The newly built hotel was magnificently opulent and way under priced for its true value. Exhaling a slow sigh of contentment, McKenzie thought to himself, 'this is going to be so good....'

Almost overnight, like a shockwave from a huge political explosion, much of North Africa and the Arab Middle East erupted in civil unrest. The flashpoint was Tunisia. Unprecedented anti-government riots brought chaos and destruction as a prelude to what would become unimaginable change.

McKenzie had to flee while he still could. He had to get out of Tunisia before the airports closed....

*   *   *

His shield came to an abrupt stop as it rammed into his assailants' 4x4 Range Rover. McKenzie took off down an alleyway like a stealth bomber, silently and with great speed, into the darkness and into the unknown....

29

McKenzie on the Run

McKenzie grew increasingly more impatient as he waited in the Mercedes for Maria to show. It was now well past their pre-arranged rendezvous time. Maybe their plot had been discovered. If so, it was inevitable that Don Pedro's henchmen would extract all the details from her and then come for McKenzie. It would be safer for him to make his escape while he could but that would mean deserting Maria.

As he pondered this dilemma, framed in the car's rear-view mirror, his eye caught something moving in the shadows. His instincts kicked in and adrenalin exploded through his body. He threw himself out of the driver's door and ducked behind a large commercial refuse bin that had been wheeled out from 'La Gaviota' just moments earlier for the nocturnal bin-men.

A bullet ricocheted off the wall behind him. McKenzie, with lightning speed, gathered his thoughts. He positioned himself behind the large container and began to push it towards the gunmen. There was a slight downward slope on the road that helped McKenzie's barricade to gather momentum. The thick rubber bin easily absorbed the bullets that flew like hail in McKenzie's direction.

Could he trust Sanjid? Could he trust Sanjid's friends who had brought McKenzie to the meeting?

Sanjid had information that was, potentially, worth a lot of money and that pay-off was his ticket to a better world far away from the political tensions and daily danger of living in Pakistan. He claimed to know of a secret arms dump that included a nuclear rocket silo. McKenzie knew that these guys were capable of committing any atrocity known to man (and a few that weren't!), even if that meant firing a nuclear bomb into any predominantly white country. They had neither morals nor scruples regarding mass murder or even single murder for that matter. McKenzie felt distinctly vulnerable…..

28

McKenzie Feels Vulnerable

To say Sanjid's house was shabby was a gross misunderstatement. The ancient outer edifice was crumbling and so too were the walls inside. It was highly unlikely that the windows had ever been cleaned. The threadbare linen curtains draped over them, although once vibrant with colour, were now sun-bleached to a monochromatic grey. They were held together by the cobwebs that generations of spiders had dexterously spun over gaping holes where countless flies were trapped in mass graves.

McKenzie stooped under the low roof in the dusty upstairs room where the meeting was to be held. Sanjid motioned for him to sit down, so McKenzie sat cross-legged on the warped wooden floor.

Sanjid had no desire to work in the brick factory that had employed his family since the day it was built. In an attempt to get out he had found himself a niche where he could run errands for the local underworld.

Unwittingly, he had found himself entangled with an Iranian-backed extremist group who, single-handedly wanted to rid Pakistan of every white infidel. McKenzie felt uncomfortable.

Shaun, a descendent of Irish immigrants from a long line of navvies, had agreed to meet McKenzie in his penthouse suite at the top of the Hilton Hotel. The thrill of lurking danger came flooding back but this time it came dressed as psychopathic madman without a conscience. McKenzie was shaking.

Shaun, a notorious arms dealer supporting ideologies that massaged his ego, had information that McKenzie needed......

27

McKenzie and the Lurking Danger

What's going on, mused McKenzie? The once familiar surroundings of his hometown, Glasgow were now strangely unfamiliar. The riverside area was completely transformed from the seedy haunts of unsavoury characters to a skyline that would rival downtown Manhattan.

As a student, McKenzie would often pass through the damp, dark and rundown side-streets of Anderston and the Broomielaw. Where low-budget prostitutes once loitered, there now stood chic, overpriced, luxury hotels and state-of-the-art office blocks.

McKenzie remembered the adrenalin-pumping thrill of lurking danger in sinister doorways. All that was now gone. The cosmopolitan city of Glasgow had become a mecca for culture vultures and a tourist attraction far removed from the territorial battlefields of razor-gangs in the 1950's. It had become a place to run to rather than from.

One thing hadn't changed however, the seedy underworld remained, hiding behind a façade of respectability and corporate success. There still death on the streets, caused directly or indirectly, by the low-life pimps and pushers. McKenzie had a meeting scheduled with one of the worst of them.

26

McKenzie and the Mercedes

McKenzie waited anxiously for Maria to show. They had meticulously planned this meeting before she helped him to escape from 'La Dama de la Noche'. Maria had decided to go back to her real father in Sao Paulo, Brazil. Together with McKenzie, they had staged his escape and arranged a rendezvous in Marbella's Old Town.

McKenzie would drive them both, in his hired car, to Malaga Airport. They would catch a flight to London's Heathrow and, from there, onto Sao Paulo. Don Pedro would be so preoccupied with finding McKenzie that they should be absorbed into the populace of Sao Paulo before he even noticed that Maria was missing.

McKenzie had left some false trails that would, hopefully, lead Don Pedro into thinking that he had driven north to France. That was what McKenzie had loudly told the man at the car hire office in Puerto Banus.

McKenzie sat quietly outside 'La Gaviota' bar, drumming his fingers on the steering wheel of the hired black Merc and he waited......

McKenzie's first meeting in Lahore didn't produce much although it was good to meet up with old friends. On his way to Multan, however, his driver detoured into Khanewal and things began to look up…..

25

McKenzie's Edge

During his time of self-imposed isolation, McKenzie had exercised less and eaten more. He had gained a few extra pounds. Not so much that anyone would notice, anyone that is, except McKenzie.

McKenzie felt that he had lost his edge. His mind was less sharp and his reactions were slow. He didn't like it, his keen instincts were fuzzy. It surely wasn't only as a result of being slightly overweight, although that would certainly contribute, no, there was something else. Isolation and a lack of interactive relationships would also be a factor. However, the one main cause for McKenzie being under par was directly related to McKenzie's distinct lack of adventure!

At heart, McKenzie was an adrenalin junkie and it had been far too long since his last fix. He was a man of action.

Now, with his project sufficiently advanced, it was time for McKenzie to start joining the dots. His first port of call was Pakistan. It was time to find out what was really going on with their nuclear arsenal…..

Miguel, as he was advised by the police, declined to comment on anything.

The remains were officially photographed and catalogued then, with blue lights flashing and sirens wailing, they were rushed over to the mortuary where a detailed post mortem would take place. The media teams followed the ambulance in hot pursuit, each one looking for their own unique slant on this headline story.

Miguel was released after hours of questioning and told to stay local. At home, clearly shaken and shocked by his ordeal, he turned on his TV and there he was, on prime time national news, overseeing the removal of the remains from his boat and all the time saying, "No comment...."

* * *

Don Pedro was in a furious rage as he sat, incredulous, in front of his huge plasma screen on board La Dama de la Noche He had a few questions of his own to ask his buffoons and they better have good answers.....

24

McKenzie Sub-Plot

Miguel radioed ahead informing the Coastguard and the Guardia Civil of his surprise catch. Before he reached the beautiful La Carihuela beach, he could see that it was packed with emergency service vehicles and, of course, the press.

Miguel ordered his small crew to unload the fish while the net, with the horrific human remains still entangled, was removed on a temporary winch set up on the sand. It was deposited into a screened off no-go area. Camera flashes popped and the TV cameras rolled, capturing every detail of the latest scoop.

The press scrum pushed microphones with their network logos attached, into Miguel's leathery face. He had seen many things during his forty-eight years of life but this took the biscuit. He was deeply affected by his grim catch. They asked him all kinds of questions....

"Where exactly were you fishing?"

"How long were you there?"

"How old is your boat?"

"What beer do you drink?"

McKenzie comes out of Hibernation

McKenzie caught his reflection in a shop window. He couldn't believe what he saw. He looked like someone who had been isolated, hidden high on a mountain or deep in a jungle or lost in a desert. His eyes stared and darted everywhere, trying to make sense of too much information. He looked like a crazy-man, cowered and shuffling, as he looked for shadows to hide in.

His hair was long and so too was his beard. He was overweight and his clothes had seen better days. His reclusive lifestyle, whilst productive, had done nothing for his image. He was feeling fearful and overwhelmed among so many people in the city.

McKenzie needed a makeover, bad. First-off, he went for a short haircut and a beard trim. He wasn't ready to lose the beard altogether, he may need it to hide behind. He couldn't stomach the small talk from the slightly camp barber, he felt detached and uninvolved with his life and lifestyle.

McKenzie had been locked into his project all winter and he felt like a bear coming out of hibernation. In his mind, he had created a complex interweave of plots and intrigue and, in doing so, he had unwittingly distanced himself from the real world of 'ordinary' people. He was now struggling to re-connect…..

In conclusion, McKenzie loathed Christmas shopping. He didn't mind buying gifts for the people he loved but he detested being dragged into the bedlam that goes with it.

22

McKenzie Goes Shopping

McKenzie pondered on how best to avoid the inevitable. What a quandary! Online shopping was infested with dangerous predators of another kind. There was nothing else for it. He would stuff his ears with cotton wool, put on his bravest smile and, behind his clenched teeth, he would jolly-well grin and bear it....

Taking a deep breath, he stepped out onto crisp snow that crunched gingerly under his shifting weight. He caught the first bus heading towards the city centre. His brain was as numbed as the frozen monochrome landscape that underwhelmingly drifted past his almost opaque, dirty bus window. Cocooned in his own thoughts McKenzie's introvert bubble was about to burst...

As soon as he entered the mall, the sound of Christmas musak grated on McKenzie's jangled nerves. Every year it was the same old, same old. It was now official: McKenzie hated Wham and Slade!

It wasn't that McKenzie disliked Christmas; he had mixed feelings about it, but he most assuredly despised the overt commercial exploitation of it. This was not some Dickensian 'bah-humbug', rather it was, plain and simply, McKenzie's opinion based on his observations.

21
McKenzie and C.A.N.T

C.A.N.T. (Campaign Against Nuclear Terror), kept a fairly loose lead on their maverick agent McKenzie. He had the kind of relationship with CANT that James Bond enjoyed with the British Secret Service. However, the main difference between the two agents was that McKenzie didn't like martinis shaken or stirred.

McKenzie had built, over the years, a comprehensive portfolio of terrorists: a 'Who's Who' of bad guys from all over the world. Now it was time to act. The clean-up operation would be global and extremely dangerous. These nuclear gangsters would fight to the death, making a nuclear war a very real threat.

Although they were spread around the planet, most of the key players knew or, at the very least, were familiar with each other. Nobody liked 'lone rangers' and, because of that, fly-by-night's didn't last long. They were a clandestine core group of shadowy figures who were disproportionately powerful for their number. Any one of them knew enough of the wrong people to blow the world apart.

McKenzie knew who they were and had met most of them face-to-face. That made him a target that not even CANT could protect....

McKenzie's mind raced back to twenty-five years ago when he had been part of a search party looking for a lost child deep in the Amazonian Rain Forest. Could it be?

"How come you have a Spanish name if you are from Brazil?" quizzed McKenzie at the risk of upsetting Maria still further. He hoped to lift a corner of the mystery that veiled Maria de las Flores' life.

"My captors took me to Colombia. Don Pedro wanted a daughter without the complications of a mother. He described exactly what he wanted and sent his men to find her. Unfortunately, his description matched me exactly and I became the daughter of the leader of Columbia's most feared drugs cartel. He renamed me and became my father ...."

For the first time McKenzie saw Maria as that frightened little girl, lost and alone.

"You talk too much McKenzie!" hollered Maria, as she threw back her raven-black hair from her angry face and stormed out of the cabin. She was annoyed at allowing herself to open-up to someone she barely knew. It was that smell: bringing memories of her early childhood. She had not smelled it for twenty-five years.....

20
McKenzie is Amazed

As quickly as she had entered, Maria left the cabin, having caused relatively little damage. McKenzie was confused and wondered what was going on. Was this part of a psychological ploy to intimidate him?

Before McKenzie had a chance to work it all out, the cabin door swung open again and Maria stood, statuesque, framed in the doorway. She was dressed to kill in her bright red mini dress. Smoke rose from an extremely long cigarette delicately held in her perfectly manicured fingers.

"You intrigue me" she purred, toying with his mind and emotions. "I have been instructed to kill you for my pleasure, but before I do, I want to know who you are." McKenzie remained silent, giving nothing away.

"There is a smell from you that reminds me of my father back in Brazil. Maybe you are my father?" She let her question hang in the air. "I hate him! He abandoned me when I was a child." Maria's lip was quivering. "He didn't come to look for me when I was taken in the jungle."

refugee, who now earned a rather lucrative living by selling secrets to the highest bidder. He was not to be trusted…..

19

McKenzie Hates Religion

The sound of the tolling bell invaded McKenzie's mind. It was seven a.m. on a sunny Sunday morning and the faithful were making their way to early mass.

Historically, France is a predominantly Roman Catholic country with a past that is steeped in religiosity far removed from the character of Jesus Christ. McKenzie believed that religion rooted in fear has bound and controlled many well meaning church-going Christians who, for the most part, are sadly unaware why they are so discontent in church.

McKenzie came from the Outer Hebrides of Scotland, a stronghold of religious control. He hated religion and that put him off Christianity although he didn't fully understand the difference between the two. Slowly, however, the revelation was beginning to dawn on him. McKenzie was soon to embark on a massive learning curve.

However, for the moment, McKenzie collected his thoughts and focussed on the day ahead. He knew that it contained potential dangers and he would need to have his wits about him. Emile, his long time friend, had set up the meeting with Youssef, a Moroccan

McKenzie was defenseless. His wrists were tied behind his back and his ankles bound together. Maria carefully positioned her expensively clad foot on McKenzie's groin and began pushing her pencil-thin stiletto into his crotch.

Maria's face broke into a crimson lip-gloss smile. "This will be such fun", she chuckled with perverse pleasure…..

* * *

As Miguel and his fishermen pulled their nets back onboard they knew that their catch was big. Their nets were heavy, but when they broke the surface they all stared horrified. There among the silvery sardines was a dead body, or at least what was left after the sharks had finished….

18

McKenzie Gets the Point

By the time McKenzie heard the key unlock the cabin door, he had maneuvered himself into a sitting position on the floor with his back against the wall. At least that way he would see what was coming.

To his surprise, it was Maria who entered, unaccompanied. McKenzie looked her up and down. As usual, she was impeccably dressed with not even a hair out of place. Her dark eyes locked onto McKenzie's upturned face. He could detect no obvious signs of emotion other than absolute self confidence. She glided over to McKenzie and asked herself out loud, "What are we going to do with you?"

McKenzie, still gagged and bound, looked into Maria's face. She stooped, grabbed a corner of the duct tape that was over his mouth and gave it a good tug. McKenzie was now able to talk. "Thank you", he said with a hint of cynicism while contorting his mouth and jaw.

"You're welcome", Maria responded with obvious sarcasm. "I want to hear you when you scream".

in another place. However, this time there was no sound of a car backfiring as in the steely cold, deserted streets of Moscow......

17

McKenzie is Hot

The car was warm, way too warm, and McKenzie was over-dressed. There had been a thick dawn mist that had rolled in from the sea and hung over the village all morning. Now, by mid afternoon, the mist had gone and the sun shone brilliantly in a cloudless blue sky. A quick scan of the people showed those who had been out-and-about since early morning; they were also overdressed. Purple overheated faces and flustered mothers milled to-and-fro with tantrum-throwing toddlers in their wake. Their, *I'm-not-giving-into-them-stare-straight-ahead* stance fooled no-one.

McKenzie opened his car door, being ever so careful not to bump the car parked next to his. Fresh, cool air flooded in. He took in a deep breath, filling his lungs to capacity and oxygenating his brain. He wedged his foot in the door to keep it open at a safe distance from his neighbour.

If the weather stayed good there would, no doubt, be a parade of scantily clad Scottish youth totally unashamed to show off their blue-white skin to the first decent rays of the year.

Was McKenzie going to have to wait much longer? He decided to step out of the car. As he stretched, he remembered another time

Multimedia screens on the walls of the building began to relay images of the in-house meeting and of other meetings taking place at the same time all over the world. People, Christians and non-Christians, were uploading and broadcasting instantaneously. Churches were showing what was being uploaded online from a battery of multimedia projectors connected to laptops. Those with a Roku Box watched live streaming on their IP TVs.

The revelation hit McKenzie like a slap on the head; this was church and he loved it.

16

McKenzie and the Digital Age

McKenzie was taken aback when the preacher walked up to the pulpit and said, "Please do not turn off your mobile phones. Leave them on and start texting and posting messages of what happens here to your friends on Facebook and Twitter. Attach photos and videos by all means."

Almost immediately, mobile phones being held aloft began flashing. Other phones were moving slowly as they panned the preacher and the congregation. "Be sure to invite the people you contact to come along to this meeting, if they can," said the preacher.

Before long, a stream of social network 'friends' began to stream into the meeting. Far from being distracting, the buzz was electrifying. The church was alive, the congregation was involved and the preacher was animated. There was some kind of activity going on everywhere.

All over the world, people were talking about the meeting that McKenzie was attending. Social networkers began to respond about what was happening in their own congregations, their home groups, whatever they were doing. Laughter and excited conversations began to ripple around the church.

Pedro's web. So far they had paid him very little attention, but McKenzie knew his time was coming.

Don Pedro's captain set a course for the marina at Puerto Banus. As they docked, McKenzie was untied from his spectator's chair and unceremoniously bundled into a cabin below deck. Still bound and gagged, he heard the door lock. They left him in a heap, face down on the Persian rug that smelled of camels, sand and Arabs.....

* * *

Miguel sailed out from La Carihuela and set his course for familiar fishing grounds in deeper water. He hoped not to snag a shark in his nets as he trawled the waters for sardines.....

15

McKenzie is Captured

Bubbles broke the surface then drifted away on the ebb tide as the weighted body sank silently out of sight to the Mediterranean Sea bed forty metres below. Back on the shore in La Carihuela, Miguel and his crew prepared their nets for a full night's fishing….

* * *

McKenzie sat gagged and bound, tied to a chair on the deck of Don Pedro Dominguez's luxury yacht, 'La Dama de la Noche'. He had watched the whole scenario unfold. Paco, the Columbian overseer, had walked into a trap and fifty kilos of pure cocaine had been seized by the Columbian authorities.

In the ensuing shoot-out, Paco had managed to escape with only minor injuries. Don Pedro made arrangements for his safe passage to Marbella in Southern Spain. After interrogation at the hands of his henchmen, Don Pedro then ordered his execution. Paco's lifeless body, suitably weighted to make it sink and stay sunk, was tossed overboard; naked and cut to attract and feed the sharks that lived in those clear blue waters.

McKenzie was a 'guest' on 'La Dama de la Noche', at the invitation of Maria de las Flores who had lured him into Don

What was happening was real but it was also supernatural. As if McKenzie was experiencing it in another dimension, a fourth dimension. For as long as this time lasted McKenzie was with Jesus, locked in an intimate encounter.

As this experience of true worship came to an end, (after how long he had no idea), McKenzie became aware of his familiar surroundings. He felt exhilarated, overwhelmed, very privileged and blessed....

14
McKenzie Visits the Fourth Dimension

McKenzie found himself caught-up in worship. He had begun to pray in a spontaneous way, but before long, joy and excitement began to well up inside him. All at once it spilled out his mouth in a cascade of words that were not his own.

McKenzie had heard about this and he had read about it. It was even mentioned in the Bible. The words came from deep inside him yet McKenzie began to have an understanding of what he was saying. He began to pray with the same effervescent joy in his own language, English.

As McKenzie continued to pray, in and out of his new language and his own native language, his spirit soared within him. He was transported to another place.

His own voice was no longer his focus of attention. Now, his focus shifted to Jesus, and as he continued he began to see Him in glorious detail. McKenzie's heart pounded and he was alive with tingling joy. Details began to appear: Jesus was smiling, His eyes were ablaze with deep compassion and immense love.

'Because the Sovereign LORD helps me, I will not be disgraced. Therefore have I set my face like flint, and I know I will not be put to shame.' (Isaiah 50:7)

That was the answer! He put on his bravest face and, like the crags of his beloved Scotland, he would weather this personal storm, seemingly, none the worse for wear….

13

McKenzie Sets His Face Like Flint

The biting wind and driving rain stung McKenzie's stubbly face. He found it exhilarating and smiled inwardly. Dressed for the weather, he leaned into the brewing storm.

'Bring it on', he said unheard, 'I'm ready!'

McKenzie had been humiliated by his peers. Initially, he was cut to the core and angry. As he planned the most diabolical revenge imaginable, a thought, seemingly from nowhere, popped into his mind. It stopped him in his tracks and he began to feel guilty about his violent and heinous machinations.

Surely there was another way? By reacting out of his hurt, McKenzie was revealing how much he had been wounded and offended. However, by not reacting but instead adopting a stoic shield of apparent unaffectedness, he would turn the table on the perpetrators.

He prayed to himself silently and asked God to help him. He remembered something he had read from the book of Isaiah:

was also frustratingly familiar. The potential was there to make this a momentous, life-changing moment for everyone; but religious ritual, cleverly cloaked in charismatic exuberance, sucked at McKenzie's energy. Instead of the tangible presence of God's glory, religion descended like a thick fog.

Many of McKenzie's most amazing life-altering encounters with God had happened outside of the traditional church setting. Now, his attention span wavered and he began to be distracted. He looked around and saw that the congregation were, for the most part, sincere and responsive. The Pastor was sincere. He obviously loved God, the Bible and his flock.

Clearly, he was looking for ways to inspire his people with the fullness of his message, so that, they would have their own personal revelation of what God was saying to each of them.

McKenzie felt the Pastor's frustration and hoped that he would accomplish what he had set out to do. His job was not enviable, it was jolly hard work. He showed great endurance and perseverance. However, it seemed that the beloved would need to be wooed for a while longer.....

12
McKenzie Looks for a Connection

McKenzie found himself at church. It was somewhere in middle England at the beginning of spring. With new life bursting out all around him, it seemed like an excellent time to make a God connection in the hope of getting things off to a good start after his winter of isolation.

From the outside it didn't look like a church building. It was a factory unit on an industrial estate. McKenzie liked that. One thing that repulsed McKenzie was overt religion. Non-religious Christianity was often difficult to find. Religion soiled true Christianity like a bad stain. Sadly, it was McKenzie's experience that religion and Christianity were bed-fellows that were difficult to separate.

McKenzie was made to feel welcome when he entered. Without much ado, he progressed into the main auditorium just as the band began to play and they were good. The presentation was good, the sound quality was good, the stage lighting was good and the projected visuals were also good. In fact, to quote the Bible…*they were very good.*

However, as the meeting progressed, the well rehearsed format morphed into a less inspired formula. It was all quite slick, but it

What was he doing lost in the merciless undergrowth of the Amazonian Rainforest? Why was he searching for someone he barely knew?

The child had vanished almost thirty-six hours ago. McKenzie's hand had shot up without his permission when the police officer made an appeal for volunteers. It could have been his little niece who was missing….it could have been him. His mind drifted back to a time when he snuggled into his mother's lap and, with his eyes closed, his mum stroked his hair as she told him this story from the bible…..

"Suppose one of you has a hundred sheep and loses one of them. Doesn't he leave the ninety-nine in the open country and go after the lost sheep until he finds it? And when he finds it, he joyfully puts it on his shoulders and goes home. Then he calls his friends and neighbours together and says, 'Rejoice with me; I have found my lost sheep.' (Luke 15:3-6).

11

McKenzie is Searching

The trees, limp and heavy after days of incessant rainfall, hung silently in the eerie stillness. The inky black sky seemed to crack open for the briefest of moments and a full moon slid out from behind a slow moving invisible cloud spilling light over the forest floor like a tremendous symphony of chiaroscuro.

Bright beams cut through the dense canopy and splashed pools of iridescence onto the damp, thick foliage of the wild forest floor. A magnificent cathedral of majestic Kapok Trees stood frozen, all-too-briefly in time, for the single strobe of the moon's glare as it flashed in the darkness.

Would they ever find what they were looking for…..?

A trickle of sweat slowly made its way down McKenzie's rigid spine. He could trace its course. Beads of perspiration congregated on his furrowed brow. The humidity was tangible. It was two o'clock in the morning and McKenzie longed for the secret solitude of his humble camp-bed back at the hut he fondly called home.

Despite the huge diversity of acts to watch, and tempting food to eat, there was one particular activity that captured McKenzie's undivided attention: the storyteller. Like a talking newspaper from the High Atlas, these specially trained and skilled orators came into the city every few months to tell their news. More popular than the snake-charmers, acrobats and fire-eaters, the crowds flocked to glean news of their distant relatives who lived secluded among the nomadic Berbers.

McKenzie was especially interested in news of Kahina; a young noblewoman who was betrothed to a ruthless Lord of the Atlas, a survivor from the infamous House of Glaoua.

He strained his ears to hear. Although the swelling crowd was hushed and hanging on every word, he still found it challenging to follow the strong Tamazight accent. Suddenly, like the sound of a finger-flick on a pure crystal glass, her name hung in the air resonating above the dusty crowd. It was as he had feared, Kahina was pregnant….

10
McKenzie Listens Hard

McKenzie sat sipping his piping-hot mint tea. There wasn't too much tea in the small chunky tumbler on account of it being crammed full of fresh mint leaves and far too much sugar. He sat at a wobbly table surrounded by an assortment of leathery faced, deeply browned and near toothless men who all looked, at least, twice their age.

They babbled away in a thick Arabic dialect to make sure they kept their conversation secret from uninvited ears. Sucking habitually on their shared hookah pipe, they took no notice of McKenzie's curious gaze.

Marrakech, nestled into the foothills of the snow-capped Atlas Mountains in southern Morocco, is a bizarre place. Sitting at this shabby little café, McKenzie had a commanding view over Djema el Fna, the main square of the old city.

Everywhere he looked, McKenzie could feast his eyes on a vast array of extraordinary delights. Alive with the buzz of tourists and locals alike, the square was a hive of activity day and night. There was never any shortage of fascinating entertainment.

The sun came back out and McKenzie allowed himself the luxury of letting his mind drift off to more pleasant places. He could hear his mother's voice calling him from far away…..

9

McKenzie's Reality Check

It started as a tiny speckle in the far, far distance, in the macro-space behind McKenzie's eyes. Sitting in his recliner easy-chair soaking up the sunshine through the window of his bedroom, he almost purred like a pussy-cat.

McKenzie inclined his head towards the wall and watched the shifting shadows and dancing lights that were refracted through the trees from the garden outside. A cloud momentarily passed in front of the sun bringing McKenzie back from day-dreaming to the stark reality of the matter in hand: why was Helga murdered and who did it?

He had no option but to walk away the night she was killed. To get involved with a murder would have complicated everything. He had been waiting on Helga returning with a contact name; a name that would take him to the leader of the Unilateral Disarmament Movement in Russia. Whoever killed Helga didn't want McKenzie to have that name.

McKenzie knew that this was more, much more, than a group of Ban the Bomb ex-hippie protesters. He wondered if he was getting in too deep.....

former kingdom of Nepal. Their sweep had already started when they raped and pillaged their way towards Kathmandu.

After the King had been deposed, the Communists had coerced their way to becoming part of the hastily formed coalition government. Since then Nepal had progressively regressed into austerity with the people struggling to eat and stay warm.

Was it possible to stop their wave of terror?....

8

McKenzie Gets High

The air at such altitude, in the foothills of the Himalayas, was incredibly thin and dry making it impossible to sweat despite the scorching heat. McKenzie's blood pressure was far too high causing his face to flush like a beetroot. His pulse was beating so hard that he thought his head would explode and his heart would burst.

The journey to Khoplang, a tiny village in the district of Gorkha in the country of Nepal, took two days walking. Much of the dirt road had been washed away by the frequent torrential rains making it heavy-going under foot for McKenzie and his Sherpa guide.

Wading through the river in full spate was not an option, even although it would have cut hours off the journey. When the driver of an old truck offered them a lift, McKenzie and his guide jumped at the chance despite the exorbitant price they had to pay for the privilege.

McKenzie had an important meeting with, Chitra, the Chief Elder of the village. Chitra had some valuable information that may just expose the Communist insurgents' take-over of the straighten his legs. Instantly, the frost attacked his ears and nose and thoughts of frostbite invaded his mind.

There was nothing else for it; he would have to go for a brisk walk in an attempt to get his circulation going. He couldn't go far because, as yet, he was unfamiliar with Moscow and its ways. Of one thing, however, he was adamant; as soon as he could, he would buy himself a furry *ushanka* to keep his head and ears warm!

The sound of a car back-firing instinctively made McKenzie spin around. There were no cars to be seen. At once, his eyes were drawn to the crumpled shape of his contact, Helga, lying just ten metres away, face-down in yesterday's snow. A crimson pool of blood oozed from underneath her, melting the snow in a sinister path towards him……

7

McKenzie Feels His Age

As McKenzie sat waiting in the car, his feet turned to blocks of ice. Even though it was minus fourteen degrees Celsius outside, he couldn't remember the cold weather affecting him this much. Maybe he was simply getting older and with each passing year the cold penetrated deeper into his bones.

McKenzie didn't like to think of himself as getting old. He still felt young at heart and his memories of bygone days were as vivid as the day they happened. He hated the cold weather and day-dreamed of the times he had lived in hotter countries.

In truth, McKenzie *was* getting older. He wasn't an old man although he struggled to do the things he used to. He was unfit. Maybe if he exercised he would feel younger, but the thought of all that hard work exhausted him just thinking about it! However, he owed it to himself and he owed it to the people who depended on him. He felt guilty about his lack of responsibility. He resolved to do better in the future…..

What was keeping her? He sighed and his breath turned to vapour. He decided to get out of the car in order to stand up and

Blood was splattered across the walls and ceiling. The illegal church was effectively stopped and the Christians were dragged out traumatised and in shock and roughly thrown into the waiting paddy wagons.

McKenzie had pushed himself into a corner squatting. He waited for the blows but they never came. As abruptly as the militia came in, they left. McKenzie was bewildered. Had the enforcers been blinded? How could they have missed him? Surely it was a miracle.....

6
McKenzie is Spared

Condensation stuck to the window like mist on a Scottish mountain. However, McKenzie was not in Scotland, he was in South East Asia, Myanmar to be precise, Mandalay City to be exact.

A drop of water left its trail and through the window blurred images of the city made indistinct shapes through the glass. McKenzie was only wearing a t-shirt and bermuda shorts but they were soaked through with sweat. He was alone for the moment but his head was still spinning from what had just happened.

The tiny, plain room had been packed with around fifty people praying. Prayers like McKenzie had never heard; loud, fervent and passionate. Almost everyone had been weeping, their faces streaked with tears, crying out to God.

Suddenly the bamboo door had burst open and at least twenty policemen brandishing clubs had rushed in. It was carnage. The sickening thuds on beating flesh, breaking bones and frenzied screaming now filled the room that had just moments before been filled with the sound of prayer.

and the waiter. The question was: who was the seducer and who was being seduced?

The whole scenario made McKenzie sick to the pit of his stomach. If he could have been anywhere else, he would have. Right now there was a job to be done. McKenzie had to delicately extract the information he had been sent to obtain and deliver it, post-haste, to his employers.

5

McKenzie and the Waiter

Maria sat down on the vacant seat at McKenzie's table, her back as straight as a poker. The slim good-looking waiter, no more than a boy, arrived instantly and slowly eyed Maria up and down. He deliberately licked his lips and almost imperceptibly pushed out his still-forming hips in Maria's direction.

'Por favor', said McKenzie, unheard. Coughing far too loudly, he said it again.

'Perdóneme', the waiter said abstractly not taking his eyes off Maria's pursed lips.

'Dos cafes con leche', said McKenzie, obviously annoyed at the distinct lack of attention he was being given. 'Ahora mismo', said the boy with the voice of a trained Hollywood actor as he drifted off in slow-motion into the café. If it was a movie, the camera would have cut from the waiter to a close-up of Maria's captivating face, her eyelids dropping coyly to conceal a delicate blush on her impeccable cheeks, then dissolving into a misty filter and cut.

However, this was not a movie set per se, it was every inch real life and in this seduction race it was neck-and-neck between Maria

that he had an aunty Moira, his dad's sister. But surely, it couldn't be her….?

"Thank you. Busy place, isn't it?" "Yes", responded McKenzie. "My name's Archie, what's your name?" As he cordially stretched-out his hand towards McKenzie.

"McKenzie's my name", he said as he warmly shook Archie's hand. "McKenzie? That's a great Scottish name, a name to be proud of. Where are you from McKenzie?"

"Originally from up north, the Outer Hebrides."

"What part? I was stationed there during the war."

"A wee island called Scalpay, just off Harris."

"Scalpay!" exclaimed Archie. "My first love came from Scalpay. You must know her, Moira McLeod?"

McKenzie was taken aback, almost everyone on Scalpay was from the McLeod clan.

"When was that?" asked McKenzie respectfully. "Och, I was just a boy, seventeen years old. Moira was only sixteen."

McKenzie quickly did the maths. This happened around seventy years ago, putting Archie in his eighties. He remembered

4

McKenzie Meets His Past

His MP4 player was out of juice, so McKenzie tuned into the noise that surrounded him. He zoned into private conversations until he found something that interested him. He was back in Scotland, in Glasgow, in a massive shopping mall that had sprung-up from nowhere since his last visit. Malls are noisy places and they are fascinating.

Nameless people, thousands of them, milled around in all directions. Every one of them had a unique story to tell....McKenzie knew that all they wanted was someone to listen. He pondered this as he sipped his Starbucks latte, casually eavesdropping into whatever conversation caught his attention in the ambience.

"Hello son, is this seat taken?" McKenzie followed the voice to a smartly dressed old man with piercing blue eyes and a recently done neat haircut. He was holding a mug of tea standing in front of the empty seat at McKenzie's table.

"No, it's yours", smiled McKenzie politely.

teeth sparkled although there was no sun. She radiated her own light.

'Steady…' mused McKenzie, convinced that Maria could read his thoughts…..

However, when Maria Lopez de las Flores appeared out of a narrow lane on the other side of the square, his heart did skip a beat. There was an air of elegance and sophistication, like twin sisters, that accompanied Maria wherever she went.

McKenzie scrutinised every inch of her as she made her way towards him. Her jet-black hair was tightly pulled back from her pale sculptured face. Her dark eyes, like mysterious deep pools and her ever-so-slightly pouting red lips, perfectly complimenting her crimson-red shawl meticulously draped from her pushed-back shoulders, like a proud matador's cape after the kill. She exuded confidence. He was going to have to tread very carefully with this one.

He stood to his feet as she approached. Maria locked her hazel eyes on McKenzie's Aryan-blue stare. Her delicately perfumed hand hovered gracefully in front of McKenzie as she waited to be greeted. He bowed slowly and taking her hand gently in his, he kissed the back of it,

'Charmed' said McKenzie, smiling broadly. 'Thank you for coming'.

'The pleasure is all mine.' Maria's melodious voice resonated from deep within her like a treasure that had been hidden until now. Her

3

McKenzie Meets Seduction

The heavy rain beat steadily down on the cathedral steps, turning the dust to mud and then washing it away. Spain in the rain – not what he was hoping for! McKenzie sat under the canopy of a café situated on one side of a very beautiful plaza and thoughtfully sipped his café con leche. Normally, he would have savoured this moment while indulging in his favourite pastime: people watching, but the cobbled plaza, now shiny and treacherous, was almost deserted.

McKenzie focussed on the drenched horse-drawn open carriage that waited in vain for tourists. Statuesque, the chestnut brown mare stood completely immobile seeming to enjoy this welcome respite and happily unaware of the unseasonably bad weather. Sun-beaten, the gypsy driver sat forlornly wrapped in a brightly coloured thin plastic poncho that caught the drips from his sodden stiff brimmed hat that, in turn, sheltered the permanent 'Ducados' cigarette burning slowly between his sardonic silent lips.

Would she keep their appointment? Was he bothered? McKenzie had developed an inherent trust in God that gave him the confidence to believe that no matter what happened, everything would work out for the best. Was he bothered? Not at all.

'What difference can you make?' he quizzed.

' I may not be able to make a difference to all of them but I can certainly make a difference to the ones I put back into the ocean!'

McKenzie's mind was made up. He would start with one person in the slums and aim to make a difference. One-by-one, he would try to help as many as he could….

2
McKenzie Makes a Difference

McKenzie stared blankly at the grotesque panorama of chaos and poverty that spread out before him. The rank smell of decay nauseated him. What could he do? Where could he start?

Njenga slum was home to around one million displaced and marginalised inhabitants on the edge of Nairobi, Kenya. Looking at the impossible task that confronted him, McKenzie remembered the story his father had told him when he was a boy.

Another boy, around the same age as McKenzie, was walking along a beach as the tide was going out. The shoreline was littered with flotsam and jetsam from the previous night's violent storm. In among the debris were hundreds of dying starfish.

The boy stooped to pick up a starfish and gently threw it back into the deeper water. As he went on his way, he continued to pick up starfish at random and throw them also into the sea. An older man, who was likewise out for a stroll, saw what the boy was doing and gruffly remarked that there were too many starfish to save, the task was impossible and the young boy would be as well to give up.

was racing so fast that it felt like it would burst out of his chest. Fear paralysed his throat as he struggled to scream out, 'Dad!'

'What is it son?'. The strong, reassuring sound of his dad's voice pierced the darkness and dissolved McKenzie's fears....

1

McKenzie Confronts His Fears

The air was so humid that McKenzie's cheap off-the-shelf spectacles slid down the greasy slope of his aristocratic aquiline nose. Almost habitually and certainly without thinking, he pushed them back up to the bridge of his nose where beads of sweat formed between his furrowing eyebrows.

At any cost, McKenzie was determined to finish his paper that he would present that afternoon to the scientific intelligentsia at the World Summit for Unilateral Disarmament in Sao Paulo, Brazil.

For a moment he was distracted. Was that a creak he heard on the well-worn stairway outside of his shabby hotel room or was his fertile mind playing tricks on him.....?

McKenzie smiled inwardly, why was he anxious? His mind went back to the time when, as an eight year old boy, he woke up during the night struggling to make sense of the worst technicolour nightmare he had ever had.

His pyjamas stuck to him with sweat, his eyes, bulging, stared wildly into the unyielding darkness that surrounded him. His heart

Group or Individual Study

The chapters of both *McKenzie* books co-relate to each other; in each book, chapter one lines up with chapter one, chapter two with chapter two....and so on. For group or individual study I have included three pertinent questions on a fresh page after each chapter of *McKenzie's Companion* leaving about one-third of the page blank under each question for the answers.

There are some completely blank pages around the middle of the book for personal notes.

With fifty chapters, at one per week, this book will take a year to complete (allowing for two weeks off).

INTRODUCTION TO THE STUDY

Thank you for purchasing this book containing *Who is McKenzie?* and *McKenzie's Companion.* I pray that you will be blessed and your relationship with Jesus Christ will be the better for it. The general purpose of each book is to take the reader on a journey into Christ.

Without Jesus Christ as our Lord and Saviour, we all lived our lives upside down and back to front as is illustrated in the unusual way these books are presented.

Who is McKenzie? introduces us to the remarkable McKenzie character. We travel the globe and enter into the fascinating world of McKenzie. It gives us an overview of his enthralling life. McKenzie is intriguing, upright, fearful but hopeful......The truth is that there is a bit of McKenzie in all of us and a bit of all of us in McKenzie.

McKenzie's Companion is a collection of short, easy to read devotionals that can be read by Christians for personal edification or by curious non-Christians as an exploration of selected scriptures from the bible. Read together, the reader will discover the scriptural context of McKenzie's scenarios in *Who is McKenzie?* and, hopefully, through that, will see how Jesus Christ can be relevant, if not essential, in their own lives.

Comments

Contact Details

TABLE OF CONTENTS

Introduction

DEDICATION

To every McKenzie both lost and found….

Who is McKenzie?

Peter Stanway

Lightning Source UK Ltd.
Milton Keynes UK
UKOW040624250712
195221UK00001B/32/P

9 780983 918677